MW00884173

Mark Twain & Me

Unlearning Racism

Calvin Pritner

Copyright

Copyright © 2021 Evamarii Johnson

All rights reserved. No part of this book may be reproduced or used in any manner without the prior written permission of the copyright owner, except for the use of brief quotations in a book review.

Hardcover: 978-1-716-34269-1

Library of Congress Number Cataloging-in-Publication Data

Pritner, Calvin

Mark Twain and Me: Unlearning Racism

viii + 133 p.

ISBN 978-1-716-34269-1

1.   BIOGRAPHY AND AUTOBIOGRAPHY/ Literary Figures
2.   SOCIAL SCIENCE/ Discrimination & Race Relations
3.   BIOGRAPHY & AUTOBIOGRAPHY/ Educators

Edited by Scott Walters
Preface by Evamarii Johnson
Published by Think Again Publications (Asheville, NC)
Printed in the United States of America

Cover photo: Calvin Pritner as Mark Twain

For Alysha, Patrick, and Christian

Table of Contents

A Note from the Editor

In addition to being my teacher, mentor, and co-author, Calvin Pritner was really a second father to me. When he passed away in December 2014, I was aware that, for several years, he had been working on a book entitled *Mark Twain and Me: Unlearning Racism*, that the manuscript was complete, and he had been looking for an agent to help him to get it published. At the time, I was too busy teaching to follow up, but when I retired in 2020, I reached out to Calvin's wife, Evamarii Johnson, to discuss the possibility of getting it into print. She sent the files from Calvin's computer, and I began to read.

The first thing I noticed was that, for anybody who knew Calvin personally, the sound of his voice was extremely clear. In his other books, like *How to Speak Shakespeare* (co-authored with Louis Coliaianni) and *Introduction to Play Analysis* (which he and I wrote together), Calvin's style was always very direct and spare, stripped of anything that wasn't absolutely necessary – all nouns and verbs nailed together in short sentences appropriate to a textbook. This book's combination of memoir and critical biography, on the other hand, is much more personal, and he allowed his sense of humor and way of telling a story to come through more clearly. That's not an easy thing to do. More than anything, I didn't want the editing process to diminish that.

Because most of this manuscript was written more than ten years ago, it doesn't reflect the struggles and tensions, nor the triumphs, of the past decade. I have not attempted to bring it up to date, not only because of its historical context as memoir, but because also the experiences described do not seem dated.

In her preface, Evamarii outlines why she thinks this book is important right now, and I agree with her completely. In the wake of so many African Americans being murdered by police and the racial underpinnings of our justice system finally being acknowledged, as well as the current rise of white supremacy, the need for white people to "unlearn racism" has moved to the forefront of many people's consciousness. Books like Robin DiAngelo's *White Fragility: Why It's So Hard for White People to Talk About Racism* and Ibram X. Kendi's *How to Be an Antiracist* have become bestsellers as people struggle to confront white supremacy, and how it underlies so much of our society. While such books can be helpful and enlightening, I see *Mark Twain and Me* as serving, in many ways, as a prologue to them, one that describes what it *feels* like to go through the process of "unlearning racism." I think this book can make this process seem less intimidating, indeed almost pleasurable, as the reader sees Calvin and Twain increase their self-awareness and understanding and, over time, become better men. As such, I think this book offers encouragement to those of us wanting to change.

Scott Walters
Bakersville, NC 2020

Preface

This book is a conversation between the author, Calvin Pritner, and you. It is born of conversations he had with himself, with his past, and with the work and life of one of our great American writers, Mark Twain. It is a conversation with memory. The topic is race and as such, it is oftentimes a difficult conversation, a sad one, a funny one — after all, Mark Twain is involved — and ultimately, a rewarding one.

This is not an academic essay on America's longstanding and ongoing problems confronting our racial history. Neither is it a book by some "woke white guy" talking to you about how to "unlearn" racism. Calvin was an honest and very humble man, genuinely interested in how we live, how we live with each other, and how we can do that better. This is a book by a man honestly exploring his history with race in this country.

Mark Twain and Me: Unlearning Racism grew out of Calvin's work on a humorous piece that he performed, "Mark Twain Traveling." The more Twain he read the more the issue of race emerged as a strong feature in Twain's writing. He decided to do a piece about Twain and race, which he called "Mark Twain Unlearning Racism." As Calvin worked on that project, the notion of examining his own history with race relations began to take hold and what had been planned as a performance piece about Twain and race became this book.

Why Twain? The genesis of Calvin's exploration began from reading Twain's works, primarily those about his travels, such as *Following the Equator* and *A Tramp Abroad*. He noticed that Twain often had something to say about race and ethnicity, often funny, many times derogatory. This led to a much wider reading of Twain's novels, short fiction, and essays, as well as many biographies and literary commentaries. He began to see that Twain's thinking and writing about race,

vi

particularly as concerned black people in America, changed over time. It looked as though a man, born in 1835 and raised in a Midwestern slaveholding family in a 19th-Century community comfortable with structural white supremacy, began to question that structure. Calvin began to see some similarities between himself and Twain. He was born 100 years after Twain, in 1935, into a Midwestern structurally-racist community. He found himself wondering whether, like Twain, had his opinions on race changed? Yes, but when, why, and how? This slender volume, this conversation, explores those questions.

Why is this important? Why now? We are still dealing with the issues about which Twain wrote and about which Calvin writes. It is important because this is the work of a regular guy like your dad, your uncle, you. It is not the work of an historian of race relations, nor a social scientist studying a culture, but rather a man who in his seventh decade was inspired to examine his own history in relation to race by, among other things, his encounter with a great writer. His journey was personal, and so stands as an example of the kind of reflection and exploration that needs to be done more often.

Calvin was an educator, a theatre historian, and the founder of a Shakespeare festival that is still in operation. He was an actor, a director, and chaired two university theatre departments. Much of his thinking was influenced by the works of Shakespeare, Clarence Darrow, and eventually, Mark Twain. This was a sophisticated, well-traveled, cultured man who enjoyed theatre, and music and baseball — especially baseball, you will find this conversation peppered with sports talk. But he was also a white man born and bred in the middle of the country at a time of accepted racial discrimination and strongly enforced segregation. He chose to explore how that breeding influenced him, damaged him, and how he changed.

Know that the N-word is found in these pages; again, we are talking about Twain and about white folk in the 20th Century talking among themselves. Both the author and the editor use the word in context, only in quotes in which it was written or spoken. Yes, it is an ugly word used only to wound, humiliate, or disregard another person or peoples, a word that is difficult to even read. It is also a part of our history and should be acknowledged in context as an emblem of historical behavior we as a nation must endeavor to unlearn.

For a few hours you have the opportunity for a lively conversation with two interesting men whose company you will enjoy. This book is serious, parts are sad and discomfiting, and parts are very funny. My hope, and I know Calvin's would be as well, is that it encourages you to read more of Mark Twain's writings and also, importantly, that you take your own journey, especially given our current cultural moment, to examine and explore your own relationship to race in our country.

Evamarii A. Johnson
New York City, 2020

"...you've got to be carefully taught."

– *South Pacific* (Richard Rodgers and Oscar Hammerstein)

Chapter One

Mark Twain & Me

"I reckon I had better black my face, for in these Eastern States niggers are considerably better than white people."
— Mark Twain letter home at seventeen (1853)

"Let's go throw some eggs at niggers."
— Cal Pritner's Kansas City teenage friend (1953)

We were cruising, three high school seniors and one junior, in a primer-coated '47 Chevy sedan, two in back, two in front. Rich, the fifth and final pickup, leapt from his front porch, yanked the car door open, tumbled into the back seat beside me, reached across to a six-pack sitting by the hump, snatched and popped a Schlitz, lifted it to his lips for what seemed thirty seconds, and, when he had no breath left, ended the gulp, filled his lungs with a chest-swelling breath and yelled out: "Lets go throw some eggs at niggers." As soon as the words were out, he reached between his legs into a brown paper bag he'd toted from home, and displayed three creamy white eggs. Laughter filled the sedan.

Dave, a junior, weeks older than I and far more streetwise, wheeled onto Leavenworth Road and headed east toward the river and the black section of Kansas City, Kansas. Conversation dodged aimlessly from "niggers," to girls, to cars, to sports, and to jobs. Girls were important to me, but I obsessed almost as much about baseball, which I was good at: All-City in Kansas City and recruited for a semi-pro team managed by a former minor-leaguer who was a Yankee "bird dog" (a scout who wasn't on salary but who maintained a relationship with the Yankee talent-scouting system). And I'd quickly fit in with the high school crowd after transferring from small-town Hartford, one hundred miles away, in the middle of my junior year.

Only a moment after we turned off Leavenworth Road onto Seventh Street, Leo, riding shotgun up front, spotted an old black man walking south, parallel to our path along Seventh. Dave eased close to the curb and slowed to the old man's pace. As we neared the ambling pedestrian, Leo leaned out the window, cocked his right arm and hurled a pair of eggs in an awkward motion unworthy of the steady infielder he was. As the eggs left his hand, he gave out a whoop and the old man glanced hurriedly to his left to see where the sound came from, then stumbled forward, touching his right hand to the side-walk, and in a single motion rose and scrambled forward. The eggs splattered harmlessly on the sidewalk, five or six feet from the old man who had regained balance. Dave floor-boarded the Chevy, made a sharp right turn at the next corner and sped away. The carload of us laughed while looking over our shoulders to be certain we weren't being tailed.

That's part of who I was as a high school senior in 1953.

Was I a racist? Yes, to the extent my racism was the face of white racism that I believe typified America in the 1950s; a racism that I'd learned from my father in Los Angeles, from his father in Kansas , and from my maternal grandfather who, on an Oklahoma summer day on his dairy farm, asked me about "the niggers in Kansas City;" the same maternal grandfather who hated FDR's integrationist wife, Eleanor Roosevelt, so much that he referred to a trip to the privy for a bowel movement as going to "Eleanor's house."

Mine was a racism that I learned from the white families and white schools and white neighborhoods that were all I'd grown up knowing. Mine was a white superiority I'd learned from the racially demeaning jokes I'd grown up laughing at and repeating, a white superiority I'd learned from everyday references to "Kikes" and "Spics," "Greasers" and "Dagos," "Chinks" and "Krauts," and of course to "Japs."

Mine was a racism I'd learned from reading the *Kansas City Star* and the *Kansas City Times*, daily newspapers that reported crimes as committed by "Robert Smith (Negro)" but never by "John Doe (White)"; a racism I'd learned from my high school history teacher who explained to us that "separate but equal" was a system that the American people and the Supreme Court had decided was good and fair.

All this lifted me to a state of righteous conviction that white people were the best people—a state of believing we were superior and we deserved it. We deserved to have the best clothes, to live in the biggest and nicest houses, and to have the best jobs that paid the most money. It was right for mayors and governors and senators and presidents to be white men. We whites were supposed to run the world.

So, is it any wonder that I can readily visualize another moment with another black man: it was my first day on the job as a laborer, repairing track for the Santa Fe Railroad just outside Kansas City. By eight-thirty the sun was scorching, and the foreman announced our first break after an hour-and-a-half's work. My companions, black and white, laid their shovels in place and stepped down the slope from track level toward a ten-gallon container, beside which sat a bucket and dipper. The black man who had been teaching me how to tamp gravel and dirt under wooden ties was the first to reach the container and bucket; he poured water into the bucket, lifted a dipper-full to his mouth and drank, after which he dipped again and turned, offering it to me. After more than fifty years, the memory of that dipper being proffered—the muscle memory of my hesitation—my near-fear, and my momentous decision to accept the man's dipper and drink, return as readily as remembering the same summer's sight of a walk-off line drive base hit off a lefthander who'd struck me out three times that night.

What I can't remember, though, is whether I felt any concern for, or connection with, the man who offered me the dipper on that blazing summer morning. I remember the dipper, the fear, the uncertainty and confusion. But I remember nothing about the man except his color. I believe that's because to me he was black and therefore unimportant. That's another part of who I was as a seventeen-year-old in 1953.

4

*****

One hundred years before that, in 1853, the boy who was to become Mark Twain left his Hannibal, Missouri, home to see the world. He found work as a printer's apprentice in Philadelphia, and subsequently in New York City from which he wrote his mother, "I reckon I had better black my face, for in these Eastern States niggers are considerably better than white people."[1]

Was this simply an isolated bit of tasteless humor? No. Days later he wrote her,

> Of all the commodities, manufactures— or whatever you please to call it—in New York, trundle-bed trash—children I mean—take the lead. Why, from Cliff street, up Frankfort to Nassau street, six or seven squares—my road to dinner— I think I could count two hundred brats. Niggers, Mulattoes, quadroons, Chinese, and some the Lord no doubt originally intended to be white, but the dirt on whose faces leaves one uncertain as to the fact, block up the little, narrow street; and to wade through this mass of human vermin, would raise the ire of the most patient person that ever lived.[2]

Was Sam Clemens—our Mark Twain—a racist? When he was seventeen, yes. When he died at seventy-four? No, at least not by the standards of his day. He'd changed. To some degree he'd unlearned his racism.

However, if those *weren't* the words of a 17-year-old racist they certainly were those of a young man who was writing at a time in American history when slavery was legal and ethnic minorities could be dismissed with casual disdain. Terrell Dempsey, in his *Searching for Jim: Slavery in Sam Clemens's World,* cites compelling evidence that the newspaper Sam and his brother together had been editing was absolutely pro-slavery, as were the other newspapers in Hannibal. So, we can say with some level of certainty that at seventeen he was a racist.

*****

Mark Twain unlearned his racism as an adult, for reasons we can analyze and hypothesize about, but that we can never declare with certainty. Similarly, I'm sure I began unlearning my racism, like Twain, as an adult; but, because I'm aware that my memory plays tricks on me, I can only hypothesize with greater specificity, albeit without absolute confidence. In other words, neither Twain's texts nor my memory are complete.

Which, of course, leads to an important question concerning this book: Why mingle the stories of Mark Twain and me unlearning racism? Why not write a scholarly volume focusing on Twain's racism? Or why not just write my own memoir and leave it at that?

There are plenty of reasons: Because racism still pervades American life more than a century after Twain's death in 1910. Because he was one of our greatest authors, and the story of his unlearning racism is both complex and compelling.

But why me? Because I grew up 100 years later in an America that still tolerated lynchings, cross burnings, job discrimination, segregated schools, and redlined housing. Because I am convinced that young people must be made aware of the past if they are to understand the present. And because the truth of America's racial past is a story that went mostly untold for a century after the Civil War, and is still being revealed only in bits and pieces. Finally, because old white guys like me have a chance to make a difference by analyzing and reporting how we taught ourselves to change. In fact, it is crucial that we do so.

I'm fascinated by Twain, by his genius, by his lifetime of self-examination, by his egotism and his greed, by his successes and his failures as a writer, husband, father, and friend, and especially by the way studying his life and work has inspired me to examine layers of my racial experience. Let's face it: I'm the hero of my own little soap opera. In my seventh decade, I'm still unlearning my racism, and I fear I'll be unlearning it until they slide me into the crematory. Despite the fact that I'm in an interracial marriage that has succeeded since 1984; that I have a grandson with an Hispanic surname; that I live in a mostly Dominican—at least ninety per cent "brown"—neighborhood; that by some people's standards, I may be thought of as being racially enlightened—despite all that, vestigial pockets of my racism still surprise, shock, and embarrass me. I'm still unlearning my racism.

In addition, my story's important if you believe, as I do, that American racism hasn't been eradicated but that it's been weed-whacked—cut off at the surface, not at the root. My experience is important if a culture's elders must remember with honesty, and admit truthfully, who we have been. Parts of my story are embarrassing, but the shameful parts are central to the justification for telling it.

I'll tell neither Twain's story nor mine in careful biographical detail; rather, I'll weave between him and me, examining key incidents in each of our stories of unlearning racism. After all, even Twain believed his autobiography, mostly dictated in his last decade, should be relatively formless. He advised:

> Start at no particular time of your life; wander at your free will all over your life; talk only about the things which interest you for the moment; drop it the moment its interest threatens to pale, and turn your talk upon the new and more interesting thing that has intruded itself into your mind meantime.[3]

This story of Mark Twain and me unlearning our racism will follow a middle path, pursuing a mostly chronological sequence, focusing on key racially oriented incidents, and using footnotes mostly when it seems important to confirm that citations are accurate.

Let me begin with a story from my own life that might illustrate why these stories, Twain's and mine, might need to be told at this point in our nation's history.

A Semester at Sea

My wife and I taught our way around the world in 1991 as Semester At Sea (SAS) faculty. The 110-day voyage's first emergency came when President George H. W. Bush attacked Iran and Saddam Hussein in Operation Desert Shield. Our original itinerary would have taken us through the Suez Canal, but given international events, it became clear that 500 American college students floating through the Gulf might be a tempting target. So, the SAS administration improvised: rather than sailing east from Nassau, Bahamas, to Morocco and on through the Suez, we diverted south from Nassau to Caracas, Venezuela; then to Salvador, Brazil; and finally, we were to sail across the Atlantic to South Africa.

Four nights out of Nassau, we docked on a starlit night at La Guira, Caracas's port city, which greeted us with a romantic mountainside view dotted with scores of lights. Morning revealed the hillside's reality: it was stacked with favelas, flimsy family shacks, many without running water, home to the poorest of Venezuela's poor, and our voyage's introduction to third-world poverty. Caracas, in preparation for Carnival, was on holiday from days of stormy political demonstrations that preceded our arrival.

Next: Salvador, Bahia—Brazil's blackest city, the port where Portuguese slave traders brought their African captives.

Salvador is just below the Equator; it's hot there in January, very hot.

Our U.S. Department of State greeter warned our 500 students of the dangers facing them if they left the ship and ventured into the city: sexual license, drunkenness, huge trio-electrico trucks blaring samba music, groups of men dressed as women, and women in string bikinis. Naturally, within hours our students were in the midst of the samba and sex that the State Department representative had warned them away from.

After five nights and days of Carnival in Salvador, we left behind the sweat, the sex, the strong beer, and the sidewalk-shaking music. But we soon learned that we were sailing south-west into a new emergency.

The Academic Dean gathered the faculty and explained our dilemma: the voyage's African specialist, the head of the University of Pittsburgh's Black Studies Program, couldn't join us at our next scheduled port, Cape Town, South Africa. Absent a specialist who could address the complications of South African politics and race relations, the administration had determined we would sail around the Cape of Good Hope and up the east coast of Africa to Mombassa, Kenya. The essence of the rationale: Kenya was a settled African nation, a long-term democracy with a hospitable government, and Kenya offered us an opportunity to experience safari.

After explaining the new plan, the Dean turned to our two black faculty members, my wife, Evamarii Johnson, a theatre faculty member, and Kesho Scott, a professor of American Studies and Sociology. Looking at the two black professors, he explained that we (terms like "shipboard community" and "faculty community" were employed) would have to depend on Kesho and Evamarii to prepare our students to visit Africa.

Heads swiveled toward the two; both were surprised, mildly shocked. Kesho spoke first: "I understand that we're in a difficult time. We have to pull together and support each other. Like you said, 'community.' But you need to understand that I'm here because I want to visit places I haven't been. I want to learn about the world. I've visited West Africa for a few days, once, but I definitely don't know the history of Africa. I'm not an historian. I'm not a political scientist. My training is in Sociology and in American Studies. I'm not prepared to teach anybody about Africa. I barely have time to prepare to teach three courses that are totally new preparations for me."

In near-unison the whole faculty ducked their heads, looking away, beginning the first awkward silence of the meeting. The Dean seemed surprised. What had he expected?

Then he turned to Evamarii, who paused, surveyed the room, then locked eyes with her colleagues: "Like Kesho, I'm here because I want to visit new places and have new experiences. My Ph.D. is in theatre history and dramatic criticism. I'm teaching one African play, it was written by a Nigerian, Wole Soyinka, and I've prepared to teach my students about him and his theatre. I'm not prepared to introduce five hundred American students to a continent I've never visited. You want Kesho and me to teach about Africa and colonialism and persecution and segregation and apartheid, and about South American and North American black folks who were brought from Africa." She paused for several seconds, then continued: "I don't teach white folks about black folks any more. I've learned they don't want to hear it from me. If they're going to hear about race, and racial history, and about how things are and how they got that way, and how things should be, they need to hear it from you, from white folks, from their fathers, their uncles and aunts, and from their white professors. If I tell the story, they'll just hear me as one more angry black woman."

Momentarily I joined my colleagues in awkward self-consciousness, but in the time it took to draw my next breath I knew she was right, and that realization serves as the impulse for this book: white guys like me must tell these stories, the good and the bad, the positive and negative. If Americans are to understand our four-century history of racism, if we're to ever make an attempt to unlearn our racism, part of the experience must involve hearing well-intentioned white guys like me, guys who were raised in an America that had been doing the wrong thing about race for centuries, guys like me who sometimes had done the wrong thing, guys like me who thought ugly thoughts, but guys who learned and changed, and are still learning and changing, trying to figure out what the right thing is and how to do it.

When we returned from sailing around the world, confronting race and racism in every country we visited in a semester's voyage, I began to read Mark Twain, first because he was a world traveler; later because he was a man who spent a lifetime wrestling with race, mostly in America, but also in Europe, in Africa, in Asia, in New Zealand and Australia, and in Ceylon and India. Reading Twain and reading biographies of him has inspired questions about my relationship to race that I would never have confronted otherwise.

In the book that follows, I'll weave in and out of Mark Twain's and my stories, focusing on our experiences of race and of unlearning racism. Twain complicates our understanding of his life by telling multiple and sometimes conflicting versions of his life story. After all, he insisted his autobiography could be published only after he was dead, because he believed we humans can tell the truth about ourselves only when we're dead. In fact, we don't know that Twain ever addressed directly the question I'm posing about him: How did he unlearn his racism? He never said: "This is how I did it." In fact, the best we can do is identify and interpret pieces of scattered evidence.

And that is true of my own story as well as Twain's.

Chapter Two

Corn-Pone Opinions

"You tell me whar a man gits his corn-pone, en I'll tell you what his 'pinions is."

— Mark Twain, "Corn-Pone Opinions" (1923)

Mark Twain's essay, "Corn-Pone Opinions," published in 1923, thirteen years after the author's death, uses "corn-pone" —a type of poor-folks food made from corn meal and whatever else happened to be available—as a metaphor for the social approval that human beings seek. In it, Twain tells a story of his 15-year-old self listening in wonder to a young black slave preaching sermons from atop his master's woodpile. Twain writes that the black philosopher's idea was that "a man is not independent, and cannot afford views which might interfere with his bread and butter." He continues:

> If he would prosper, he must train with the majority; in matters of large moment, like politics and religion, he must think and feel with the bulk of his neighbors, or suffer damage in his social standing and in his business prosperities. He must restrict himself to corn-pone opinions—at least on the surface. He must get his opinions from other people; he must reason out none for himself; he must have no first-hand views.[4]

Twain claims in the essay that we get our morals, our religion, our table manners, our politics, in short—all of our ideas and our beliefs—from others, because we value more than anything the self-regard that we gain through the approval of our friends, neighbors, and business associates. The result, Twain asserts, is "conformity," not by "calculation and intention," but unconsciously. We believe we're thinking originally, but in reality, our self-interest lies in being smiled upon by our friends; we want to hear the precious words "he's on the right track," and we'll dump life-long principles in the street, our consciences along with them, in order to gain the approval of others. Twain goes on:

"Mohammedans are Mohammedans because they are born and reared among that sect, not because they have thought it out and can furnish sound reasons for being Mohammedans; we know why Catholics are Catholics; why Presbyterians are Presbyterians; why Baptists are Baptists; why Mormons are Mormons; why thieves are thieves; why monarchists are monarchists; why Republicans are Republicans, and Democrats, Democrats. We know it is a matter of association and sympathy, not reasoning and examination; that hardly a man in the world has an opinion upon morals, politics or religion which he got otherwise than through his associations and sympathies. Broadly speaking, there are none but corn-pone opinions.[5]

Did Twain believe this? My reading of him is that he not only believed it, he lived it and he wrote it. He sticks to it like it's flypaper. My next question, then, is do I believe it? Do I believe that what we in the theatre call the "given circumstances" of our lives—the social, political, historical, and personal aspects of existence into which we are born—shape our attitudes and our beliefs? And that even when we change our attitudes, it is because we're chasing more corn-pone—more approval? It's sure hard to argue.

My dad was racist, and his father before him was racist. They showed it in different ways, but there's no doubt they were racist.

By seventeen, I'd taught myself to be a racist, too. While Dad and Grandpa Pritner modeled it, I'd also taught myself. At seventeen, my corn-pone came from fitting in, especially at school where my self-esteem came from being one of the "in crowd." Having moved from small-town Hartford to suburban

Kansas City, it felt so good to be part of the popular group that I fit my beliefs and behavior to them – and as I peer into my memory bank, looking back fifty-some years, the nadir is the evening we celebrated our white privilege by throwing eggs at an old black man.

*****

Depending on the context and who I'm addressing, I tell folks either that I grew up on a dirt-poor Kansas farm or that I grew up as a Los Angeles street kid in what is now called South Central. Actually, it was both. My parents, Ward and Losson, were life-long deaf people. The family story was that they thought I should spend time on the farm with Dad's parents, Milt and Hetty. So, I grew up partly in a deaf culture, partly in a hearing one; partly with Ward and Losson in a working class LA environment, partly with Milt and Hetty on a thirteen-acre Kansas farm stocked with a cow and several dozen chickens, a mile and a half from Hartford, a town of less than five hundred people.

My dad was born in 1903 and educated at the Kansas State School for the Deaf at a dreadful time in deaf education: oralism was then the way hearing people believed the deaf should be taught, rather than sign language. He and Mother bemoaned their frustration with being taught to lip-read, he at the Kansas school, she at the Oklahoma School for the Deaf: "It was impossible," Mother complained of the oral-only teaching, "I couldn't understand anything." Sixty-five years later, their eyes still reflected their resentment; clearly they hated it. I've read that the verbal achievement of deaf people my parents' age was equivalent to the average hearing person's fourth grade education. Whether that's accurate or not, Dad's intelligence wasn't average; he had always been able to read and understand the sports pages, and he paid attention to national and world news through the newspaper. He was quite literate.

But he was also a race-hater.

*****

In the summer of 1946, my friend Darrel and I took an electric trolley and a city bus from our neighborhood in South Central Los Angeles to Hollywood to "watch" the radio broadcast of a baseball game. The studio was filled with "listeners" who sat in folding chairs arranged so we could see the announcer. The play-by-play announcer sat at a table on a raised platform, a microphone hanging from a stanchion that enabled a nearby engineer to swivel and point the mike. Beside the table was a ticker tape machine that fed pitch-by-pitch information to which the announcer added details. For example, a game could be going on all the way up the Pacific Coast, with the Los Angeles Angels or the Hollywood Stars playing against the Seattle Raineers of the AAA Pacific Coast League. One engineer swiveled the mike; another person controlled recorded crowd noise. Beside the announcer was an upright thin metal pole that was bent at the top in a right angle. Hanging from the angled metal was a small wooden baseball bat perhaps eighteen inches long. The announcer rapped a metal stick against the bat to imitate the crack of bat against ball; of course, striking the metal against the bat cued the engineer to swell the crowd noise. As vivid as the memory of that scene remains, sixty or so years ago, for the life of me I can't figure out why we were sitting there watching a ball game being broadcast from ticker tape information. Listening at home on the radio? Yes. Watching it? No.

Breaking from play-by-play of the game, the broadcaster announced that Jackie Robinson, currently playing for Brooklyn's farm team in Montreal, would be going to spring training with the Dodgers under a contract that made it likely he would be joining the big league team next spring. There was a buzz around the room. I recall that most people in that room were surprised and that they didn't like what they'd heard.

Neither did my dad.

When Robinson finally entered Major League Baseball, Dad was depressed for weeks. He literally sat in our tiny studio apartment on South Broadway Place, over a Korean Store in South Central Los Angeles, in a threadbare chair, in the dark with shades pulled down, running his thumb and forefinger down his nose.

I was twelve. I asked, "Why are you sitting here like this?"

Dad was forty-two, an athletic man, trim, and muscular, physically fit partly because he'd gladly given up full-time work when he was laid off from the aircraft industry laborer's job he'd held from 1943 through 1946. Instead, he caddied at a Hollywood golf course, sometimes telling me of tips he got from stars like Don Ameche, Bob Hope and Bing Crosby. "It's better to work outdoors in the sun. I like to carry two bags of golf clubs and walk fast ahead of the players, looking for their golf balls."

But that day he was sitting in the semi-darkness. When I came in, I asked what was the matter. He said, "I feel blue. So sad."

"Why?"

"It's terrible for a Negro to play baseball," he replied. I think if he had been speaking orally instead of finger spelling, he would have said "nigger." The sign he and Mother used for black people involved placing the forefinger and middle finger over the tip of the nose, pressing down, flattening it, and wriggling the fingers from side to side. As a boy I thought nothing of the gesture, but later, especially after my wife, Evamarii, who is African American, observed and commented on it, I read it as an obviously uncomplimentary imitation of the relative flatness of some black people's noses.

Even at age eleven and twelve, despite my lack of awareness of America's and Major League Baseball's apartheid practices, I knew Robinson's playing in the big leagues was important to lots of people. Perhaps, though, those people didn't sit in the dark and stroke their noses in depression.

Boyhood memories of race and Dad connect inevitably to sports. He was a devoted fan of the University of Southern California Trojan teams. He held season tickets for USC football games. Unlike the racially integrated cross-town University of California–Los Angeles Bruins, the USC Trojans had no black players. Before World War II, UCLA had spawned both Robinson, a multi-sports star, and the football star, Kenny Washington, who went on to play for the Los Angeles Rams, and was among the earliest black players to integrate the National Football League.

From 1947 to 1949 I was one of two batboys for the USC baseball team. My first year, USC lost the Pacific Coast Conference baseball championship to the University of California–Berkeley Bears led by Jackie Jensen who later starred for the Boston Red Sox. The next year, the Trojans won their conference and went on to win the NCAA championship.

In 1949, we played a spring training game against the Cleveland Indians team that included Larry Doby and Luke Easter, both of them former Negro League stars. Doby, the first black man to play in the American League, had broken in the preceding summer. Before the game, Doby's presence generated whispered comments from players, coaches, and fans who wondered, "Does he deserve to be a major leaguer?" That day he hit the longest homer I'd ever seen; it may have been over 500 feet because it cleared the wall in center field at the old Bovard Field—it cleared the center fielder, cleared a running track behind the center fielder, and disappeared behind a wall thirty feet or more beyond the track. Everyone in the ballpark knew when the ball sailed straight and low over the Bovard Field center field wall that Larry Doby was for real. Eventually he was elected to the National Baseball Hall of Fame in Cooperstown, NY.

Dad's abhorrence of black people was devoted and nearly life-long. As a boy in Los Angeles I never learned to swim because he didn't want me to go into our neighborhood pools swimming with black people. Because the Los Angeles public school system faced impending racial integration, he wanted me to go to school in Kansas. So, for eighth, ninth, tenth grades and half of the eleventh I lived with Milt and Hetty and attended Hartford schools. I remember being told that no African American (the speaker probably used the "N" word) had ever been allowed to stay overnight in Hartford. True? I don't know, Hartford is not listed among the "sun-down towns" in Kansas, but there were no black people in town or on the surrounding farms. In fact, I was twenty-five years old and in the Navy before I ever had a conversation with a black person. I got my corn-pone from my parents and my grandparents, and they had no interest in my being associated with black people.

Milt and Hetty (Grandpa and Grandma Pritner) were born, raised, and wed in Riley County, Kansas, where they owned a drug store. There's a photo of Milt standing behind the soda counter, and he looks the epitome of "proprietor" in that photo. Eventually, they sold the store, and bought 120 acres of farmland which they farmed until 1944 when a series of angina attacks ended Milt's days as an active farmer. They moved then to a thirteen-acre farm on a gravel county road a mile and a half from town, where they kept forty to fifty chickens and a Jersey cow. After employing a hand-turned separator, they sold the cream.

In retrospect, the pittance they must have gotten from selling the cream is an indicator of how careful they had to be with their money. We shared the leftover skim milk with the chickens whose eggs Grandma and Grandpa sold. Fried chicken was a luxury that made up dinner only on special occasions. After all, Milt and Hetty were so poor that on Saturdays in Emporia, they bought a weeks's bag of day-old bread that we ate and shared with the livestock. There was no running water in the tiny farm house, and we brought electricity into the house in 1948 after years of reading by kerosene lamplight. My earliest radio memories are of a wooden, battery-powered Philco radio, that Milt, Hetty and I sat beside, listening to President Franklin Delano Roosevelt's World War II fireside chats, fifteen minute daytime soap operas (*Ma Perkins*, *Stella Dallas*, and *One Life to Live*), and to the right-wing view of the news from Fulton Lewis, Jr., a pro-McCarthyite who railed against Communists in the U.S. State Department. As a ten-year-old, I believed him whole-heartedly.

Skim milk, day-old bread, kerosene lamps, and all, I loved living with Grandpa and Grandma Pritner.

But there is a sour memory of racism from the summer of 1946 or 1947: Milt, Hetty, a male guest, and I are sitting at the dining room table of the little house on the thirteen-acre plot. The adults trade jokes at the table, mostly stories ridiculing city folks: the guest had become a city man, but he shared rural roots with Milt and Hetty. As the stories are shared, Milt tells of someone being fooled into believing Oleo, a brand of margarine, was real butter. There's another story Milt tells about a city person pronouncing the word "potatoes" with three syllables, and the farmer realizing later that the "darn fool meant taters." This was followed by a story about the city dude asking for onions; after he leaves, the farmer says to his wife, "I bet it was 'ingins' the darned fool wanted." Of course the jokes are corny, but laughter and good humor spread among us. Then Grandpa tells the capper: a story of Rastus, and his "nigger" friend who are hungry and searching for food. Rastus's friend yells out "Come here Rastus. I done found a big fat cigar butt." Rastus replies "Go 'way boy, I got some fresh puke here, with raisins in it!"

I knew nothing of racism or ethnic sensitivities. It was just the way white folks I knew talked about black people. Today, of course, the horror of my grandfather, the most beloved man of my youth, telling that ugly, stupid, racist story hangs before me, perpetually shaming him and me.

There's another memory, nowhere nearly so painful, but nevertheless curious and nagging and bothersome. I was a teenager, fourteen or fifteen, attending Hartford High School. Somehow, possibly at school, I'd learned how the Ku Klux Klan had lynched and terrorized blacks, and how the Klan's activities had been tolerated by white Americans. I realized these things had happened in Grandma and Grandpa's lifetimes, so I wanted to tell them about what I'd learned and ask them about these shameful times and horrid events.

As I visualize the day, Grandpa, Grandma, and I stand in the driveway, near the faded green 1937 Chevrolet sedan that is the only car I remember them owning. We form a triangle in the gravel driveway, three or four feet from each other, and there are spirea bushes immediately behind them, the tiny white house to one side in the background, the tin-roofed garage to the other side, and the faded red barn tipping slightly in the background. I remember none of my words, but I must have expressed amazement that white people had treated black people that way.

They glanced meaningfully at each other, and then looked at me. Then Grandpa spoke a sentence that I'd rather not remember: "Well, the Klan did a lot of good things, too."

"What?"

"They did things that had to be done and they took care of people. They helped people who needed help."

The darting look Milt and Hetty shared, and his response still cast a shadow in my memory. I've worried over Grandpa possibly being a former Klansman. Was the feud he maintained with Mr. Becker, the German-accented farmer across the road, connected to this? How complicit were Grandpa and Grandma in Dad's plan to get me out of Los Angeles before I "had to" go to high school with black students in Los Angeles? When I try to think through the 1940s racial atmosphere in Hartford, I connect only to a conversation with a schoolmate who explained to me (after all, I was a kid who spent part of each year in California and didn't know Hartford's traditions): "Niggers can come through here, but we don't let 'em stay overnight."

There's no evidence of Milt and Hetty having associations with pro-Klan organizations. The Klan, at its apogee of power in Kansas in the 1920s, was especially devoted to anti-Catholic and anti-Jewish activity. After all, there were few black residents in Lyon County. So I assume my grandparents' racism was characterized more by passive contempt and an ugly attitude of white superiority than by active hatred.

Nonetheless, I was raised by racists whose own words indicated that they viewed the Klan positively: "They did things that had to be done and they took care of people. They helped people who needed help."

*****

Twain grew up in pro-slavery Hannibal, about 300 miles east of my grandparents' farm and of course, he supported slavery; after all, his corn-pone came from a com-munity that coalesced around slavery as a rightful privilege of white masters to impose upon black laborers.

We know little about either his racial attitudes or behavior during the next phase of his life: his time on the Mississippi River, first as a cub pilot, and later as a full-fledged steamboat pilot (1857-1861). His most self-disclosive account of his relationship to the Civil War comes in a mostly humorous but partly serious piece, "The Private History of a Campaign that Failed" (1885), which begins by recounting how, soon after South Carolina seceded from the Union, he and a "pilot-mate" each argued his pro-Union point of view as they traveled south down the Mississippi and then, a month later in New Orleans, each in turn argued that he was a rebel. He goes on to report that, after the war shut down private traffic on the Mississippi, he was forced to abandon piloting and went home where he joined the Marion Rangers, a rebel-sympathizing militia company that Twain finally abandoned after possibly killing a man with a night time rifle shot. In retreat, he continues, he came pos-sibly within a few miles of a young Union Colonel who went on to become General Ulysses S. Grant.[6]

In 1861, with the river closed to private traffic, and soldiering having quickly lost its appeal, Twain accompanied his brother Orion to the Nevada Territory where Orion served the territorial government. Twain tried the silver prospector's life, but he eventually found his way into humorous writing, mostly as a newspaper man in Nevada and in California. A few lines from a letter he sent the Virginia City Nevada *Territorial Enterprise* in 1865 describing a San Francisco Independence Day parade demonstrate his continued, if somewhat ironic, insensitivity toward blacks:

And at the fag-end of the procession was a long double file of the proudest, happiest scoundrels I saw yesterday—niggers. Or perhaps I should say "them damned niggers," which is the other name they go by now. They did all it was in their power to do, poor devils, to modify the prominence of the contrast between black and white faces which seems so hateful to their white fellow-creatures, by putting their lightest colored darkies in the front rank, then glooming down by some unaggravating and nicely graduated shades of darkness to the fell and dismal blackness of undefiled and unalloyed niggerdom in the remote extremity of the procession. It was a fine stroke of strategy—the day was dusty and no man could tell where the white folks left off and the niggers began.[7]

Twain had left Nevada City the previous year because he'd gotten in deep trouble for a notably misguided humorous article suggesting that a fundraising effort for a legitimate St. Louis charity was, in fact, for an organization supporting miscegenation. Although he acknowledged in a letter to his sister-in-law that the miscegenation accusation was a hoax and that its unintended printing was the result of drunken carelessness, the dispute led to his issuing a challenge to a duel that he narrowly avoided fighting. The matter ended when Twain made an embarrassed, brisk departure from Virginia City and headed to San Francisco.

Similarly, his first big seller, *The Innocents Abroad,* the story of his 1867 excursion aboard the Quaker City, a ship bound from New York to Europe and on to the Holy Land, builds some of its humor on prejudice toward brown-skinned foreigners. After crossing the Atlantic, before touching land in Europe, the ship docked in Portugal's Azores Islands. Twain writes that "a swarm of swarthy, noisy, lying, shoulder-shrugging, gesticulating Portuguese boatmen" came aboard. "The group on the pier," he continues, "was a rusty one—men and women, and boys and girls, all ragged and barefoot, uncombed and unclean, and by instinct, education and profession beggars."[8]

Twain's second big-seller, *Roughing It,* was his account of traveling by stagecoach to the West, mining and newspapering in Nevada and California, and traveling to the Sandwich Islands (islands in Hawaii). Like its predecessor, *Roughing It* often bases its humor in ethnic stereotypes. A passage about the Goshute tribe displays contempt for American Indians that he never recanted:

From what we could see and all we could learn, they are very considerably inferior to even the despised Digger Indians of California; inferior to even the Tierra del Fuegans; inferior to the Hottentots, and actually inferior in some respects to the Kytches of Africa. Indeed, I have been obliged to look the bulky volumes of Wood's *Uncivilized Races of Men* clear through in order to find a savage tribe degraded enough to take rank with the Goshutes. I find but one people fairly open to that shameful verdict. It is the Bosjesmans (Bushmen) of South Africa. Such of the Goshutes as we saw, along the road and hanging about the stations, were small, lean "scrawny" creatures; in complexion a dull black like the ordinary American Negro; their faces and hands bearing dirt which they had been hoarding and accumulating for months, years, and even generations, according to the age of the proprietor; a silent, sneaking, treacherous looking race; taking note of everything, covertly, like all the other "Noble Red Men" that we (do not) read about, and betraying no sign in their countenances; indolent, everlastingly patient and tireless, like all other Indians; prideless beggars—for if the beggar instinct were left out of an Indian he would not "go," any more than a clock without its pendulum; hungry, always hungry, and yet never refusing anything that a hog would eat, though often eating what a hog would decline; hunters, but having no higher ambition than to kill and eat jackass rabbits, crickets, and grasshoppers, and embezzle carrion from the buzzards and coyotes; savages who, when asked if they have the common Indian belief in a Great Spirit, show something which almost amounts to emotion, thinking whiskey is referred to; a thin, scattering race of almost naked black children, these Goshutes are, who produce nothing at all, and have no villages, and no gatherings together into a strictly defined

27

tribal communities—a people whose only shelter is a rag cast on a bush to keep off a portion of the snow, and yet who inhabit one of the most rocky, wintry, repulsive wastes that our country or any other can exhibit.

The Bushmen and our Goshutes are manifestly descended from the selfsame gorilla, or kangaroo, or Norway rat, whichever animal-Adam the Darwinians trace them to.[9]

Obviously, Twain counted on readers who shared his contempt for American Indians.

But there are seeming contradictions in Twain's behavior regarding race that lead one to question his true opinions.

About the time he started writing *Roughing It* (1869), he was seeking the hand in marriage of Olivia Louise (Livy) Langdon, daughter of Jervis Langdon and Olivia Lewis Langdon. Livy was the sister of Charles Langdon, with whom Twain had sailed on the Quaker City excursion. Jervis was a self-made man who started as a storekeeper, succeeded in the lumber business, and achieved wealth in the coal trade. Jervis later loaned Twain, now his son-in-law, most of what it cost Twain to buy part-ownership of the *Buffalo Express*; in addition, the Langdons surprised the newlyweds with a furnished brick house, stable, and carriage on a fashionable street in Buffalo.

The Langdons were ardent abolitionists who had been active before the Civil War in the Underground Railroad, helping slaves escape to Canada. They also had hosted overnight the great black writer, speaker, and former slave, Frederick Douglass.

So Twain, now getting his corn-pone from abolitionist in-laws, seems to have begun thinking in a new way. He took care to use the word Negro when speaking in his writer's voice, using "nigger," in quotes, to suggest the offensive term is a Southerner's and not his own. In an essay entitled "Only a Nigger," unsigned but attributed by scholars to Twain, he reports on a lynching in Mississippi and uses irony to condemn the South and lynching. Writing that an innocent Negro man had been lynched for "ravaging" a white woman, he declares with heavy irony:

> Ah, well! Too bad, to be sure! A little blunder in the administration of justice by Southern mob-law; but nothing to speak of. Only "a nigger" killed by mistake—that is all. Of course, every high-toned gentleman whose chivalric impulses were so unfortunately misled in this affair, by the cunning of the miscreant Woods, is as sorry about it as a high-toned gentleman can be expected to be sorry about the unlucky fate of "a nigger." But mistakes will happen, even in the conduct of the best regulated and most high-toned mobs, and surely there is no good reason why Southern gentlemen should worry themselves with useless regrets, so long as only an innocent "nigger" is hanged, or roasted or knouted to death, now and then.[10]

Thus, by age thirty-five, Mark Twain had transformed himself from a seventeen-year-old, pro-slavery racist printer's apprentice and sometime newspaper editor, to a Nevada and California miner and journalist who unsuccessfully dodged racial controversy, to a nationally known author and pros-perous editor writing in opposition to Southern lynching. His culture, his family, his friends, and his employment seem to have affected his writing and thinking about race.

Chapter 3

New 'Pone, New 'Pinions

"I can't remember having a single conversation
with a black person before entering the
Navy at age twenty-three..."
– Calvin Pritner

"Aunt Rachel, how is it that
you've lived sixty years and never had any trouble?"
– Mark Twain, "A True Story Repeated
Word for Word as I Heard It" (1874)

A former colleague, one of the great teachers I've known, maintained that, "To teach is an intransitive verb. " For those who haven't visited a grammar class recently, an intransitive verb indicates reflexive action—intransitive verbs don't take an object. My colleague's idea was we don't teach others—we teach ourselves. Teachers direct us toward information; they offer us feedback about how we're doing; they suggest alter-native solutions to problems we're facing; they don't so much teach us as they guide us to teach ourselves.

My parents experienced such a moment when, in 1984 after my first marriage to Jackie had ended in divorce, I married Evamarii, who, as I mentioned previously, is African American. I wrote to them, telling them about her, and ex-pressing my hope they would welcome her. Because I wasn't sure how they would react, I followed up on the letter by driving to Kansas City alone to visit them.

I'd been in their apartment five or ten minutes when, in a tearful sign language frenzy, my mother screamed, "It's terrible for you to marry a Negro (her fingers flattened her nose). I wish it was like it was before when you were married to Jackie. I always loved Jackie because she was good to me. Jackie loved me. This is terrible. Who will take care of us? Jackie would love me and take care of me. This is awful!" Dad sat observing her explosion, choosing not to comment. I was mildly shocked. It was Mother, who had never seemed to care much about race, for whom Evamarii's race was important. From Dad, the race-hater, nothing. In fact, he came to like her a good deal. He smiled happily when we visited.

So what might have caused my father's change of attitude, at least in regard to Evamarii? Well, by the time she came into his life, he saw me as the "good son"—valued me enough, apparently, to set prejudice aside. In addition—and this also likely plays into his change—Mother had begun abusing him physically, so Evamarii and I were literally his source of protection against her dementia-fueled fear, paranoia, and anger. Like Twain, his attitudes changed once his situation changed.

*****

Winning Livy Langdon's hand in marriage was among Mark Twain's greatest achievements. As a young man out West, Sam had been (to borrow the title of one Twain biography) a "Sagebrush Bohemian," first as a miner and then a journalist who lived a life that frequently involved drinking, carousing, and hanging out with friends who shared his life-style.

So when Livy's wealthy, upper-middle class, near-Victorian family began inquiring about Sam's character and suitability as a son-in-law, those who responded as references didn't speak positively. Surprisingly, his winning card was Jervis Langdon, Livy's father, a generous man who apparently looked into Twain's heart and saw love for his delicate and beautiful daughter. And that was enough for him.

Livy and Sam married on February 2, 1870; six months later, Jervis Langdon died and a year later, Twain sold his interest in the *Buffalo Express* and moved to Hartford, Connecticut. His new neighborhood, Nook Farm, was comprised of many former abolitionists. Indeed, the leading literary figure among the collection of pro-abolitionist celebrities and their relatives was Harriet Beecher Stowe, the author of *Uncle Tom's Cabin*, and the sister of one of America's leading abolitionist ministers.

So while Twain was initially by no means Nook Farm's leading celebrity, he was nevertheless a nationally known author who was married to the daughter of a prosperous family. Now the former racist, miner, sagebrush bohemian, and frontier journalist whose miscegenation joke had motivated his quick exit from Nevada was getting his corn-pone, in part, from association with respectable Nook Farm authors and religionists who had supported abolition and who had been staunch Union supporters in the war. Part of his corn-pone also came from his family associations in Elmira where Jervis Langdon had passed on an estate estimated at a million dollars to be divided among his widow, his son Charlie, his daughter Livy, and an adopted daughter, Susan Crane.

Livy's mother stayed on in the family's Elmira home, while Charlie dealt with the family's investment interests. Livy's sister, Susan, and her husband Theodore maintained a home in Elmira but also inherited Quarry Farm, a property outside Elmira that they developed following the guidelines of the "picturesque" style of land and building development. Twain, Livy, and eventually their children spent summers at Quarry Farm, where he worked on the books that made him famous during the seventies and the eighties, among them: *The Adventures of Tom Sawyer*, *A Connecticut Yankee in King Arthur's Court*, *The Adventures of Huckleberry Finn, and The Prince and the Pauper*.

To furnish Twain the solitude he required for writing, the Cranes built, about one hundred yards from the Quarry Farm house, an octagonal single-room structure that served as his writing studio. Each morning, after a light breakfast, Twain walked to the studio where he wrote until late in the afternoon. Evenings, he occasionally read aloud from his current writing project with family and servants surrounding, listening to the world-famous author.[11]

Between his fashionable and prosperous life in Hartford's Nook Farm, where he eventually built a luxurious and distinctive family home, and his summers at Quarry Farm, Twain found a life of friendship, admiration, success, luxury, and achievement. It is of little wonder that, getting his corn-pone this way, he was in many ways, including his racial attitudes, a new man.

Despite the influence of Twain's wife and her family, Twain's process of unlearning racism was inconsistent at best.

In 1869, after he had achieved national notice from his irreverent account of traveling to Europe and the Holy Land onboard the Quaker City, Twain initiated a Boston meeting with William Dean Howells, the assistant editor of America's leading literary magazine, the *Atlantic Monthly*. The meeting began a life-long friendship between two literary giants of their time. In 1872 Howells reviewed Twain's *Roughing It*, and he praised it, to which Twain responded with a letter, a sentence of which provides one of his better-known and most notorious quotes relating to race. Twain wrote of the review: "I am as uplifted and reassured by it as a mother who has given birth to a white baby when she was awfully afraid it was going to be a mulatto."[12]

Why would Twain—newly entered into Hartford respectability, in correspondence with an executive at a leading Northeastern, racially enlightened publication—be so indelicate even with a friend? A simple guess: he thought he was being funny, in much the same way he thought he was being funny when he wrote about miscegenation in Nevada, and in the same way Grandpa Pritner was being funny by telling Rastus jokes. Apparently, Twain believed private communication among white folks licensed a sort of privileged indiscretion. Nor was this the last time in his letter-writing career that private verbal offensiveness revealed his attitude of casual and unselfconscious white racial superiority.

After he'd entered the Eastern upper crust, Twain seems to have avoided publicly using obvious racial slurs, especially the "N-word." But as late as the 1890s, he used it in his notebooks and in private correspondence for "humorous" effect. We might say Twain judged where he was getting his corn-pone, and used racial humor accordingly.

Stated simply, Mark Twain was contradictory in the way he wrote about race, and the contradictions continued for a lifetime. Contrast the insensitivity of his "mulatto" comment to Howells in 1872 with his most sensitive treatment on race in a piece Twain submitted to Howells less than two years later entitled, "A True Story, Repeated Word for Word as I Heard It." Howells printed it in 1874 with enthusiasm for its humanity: "The rugged truth of the sketch leaves all other stories of slave life infinitely far behind, and reveals a gift in the author for the simple, dramatic report of reality which we have seen equaled in no other American writer."[13]

To put Howells's judgment of Twain's "True Story" in context, it is worth noting that in 1874, less than ten years after the Civil War's end, Northern publishers had begun taking new interest in work by Southern writers who stressed the "loyalty" slaves had shown to their masters before and after the war. According to William L. Van Deburg, "Whether the story was set in the calm, prosperous days before the war or in the chaotic atmosphere that followed, blacks were portrayed as dependent upon and supremely loyal to their white folks." Throughout the 1870s and into the 1880s, according to Van Deburg, the South became an increasingly popular setting for fiction in which antebellum slaves were depicted in a fashion that might leave readers questioning the necessity of the war."[14] Even though Twain's concern for accuracy of dialect was typical of the epoch's treatment of American black persons in popular literature, the essay in no way can be thought of as supporting slavery.

"A True Story" was inspired by Twain's real-life conversation with Mary Ann Cord (the tale's Aunt Rachel), who worked for Susan Crane at Quarry Farm. Tom Quirk, in his book on Twain's short fiction, recounts that Twain's sister-in-law, Susan Crane, initiated the event that led to Auntie Cord's telling Twain her story. Apparently Clemens had claimed that his experiences of living among black people in Missouri had given him insight into their customs and ways of living. Susan Crane was sufficiently unconvinced of his expertise that she urged him several times to ask Auntie Cord to tell him her story, and Twain demurred, more than once.[15] Finally, one summer night in 1874, sitting and talking on the Quarry Farm porch, Auntie Cord laughed deeply, as was her wont, inspiring Twain to ask the sixty year-old servant, "Aunt Rachel, how is it that you've lived sixty years and never had any trouble?"[16]

Initially Auntie Cord paused, making certain Twain (the story's "Mr. C––"), was in earnest. She then proceeded to tell of her having grown up in a Virginia slave family, of being happily married and having seven children, and of the family's being transported in chains to a slave market in Richmond where she, her husband, and her children were sold and separated from each other. In her desperation, she struggled to hang on to her youngest, Henry, but she was beaten into submission with chains. She lost them all.

During the Civil War, with her owner away serving as a Confederate officer, she and his other slaves escaped, freeing her to become a cook for the Union forces. Still pining for her youngest, Henry, who had told her, as he was forced away from her at the auction, that he would grow up and someday return to her, she asked the officers for help in locating Henry. Then, at a military dance, she recognized and was reunited with her son.

The story, a powerful testimony to the stature of black women in relationship to their families, destroys the notion of slaves as being too uneducated and too dependent on whites to act forcefully in their own behalf. Auntie Cord's description of the slave auction, with its brutality, its chains and beatings, and its destruction of the slaves' families, challenges the entire pro-slavery version of history. Auntie Cord tells of no gentle plantation owners; there are no benign masters. There are no slaves clinging to their masters, none loyally protecting the plantation until the master returns from battle. As soon as she could, as soon as her town was overrun and defeated, Auntie Cord went to the Union side where she sought and received protection, support, and freedom.

It seems hypocritical, I suppose, to utter offensive racist remarks in private while in public presenting stories that push against the narrative of racism, and yet that is the constant struggle for those of us unlearning our pasts.

*****

Both my father and Twain changed their attitudes to reflect the values of those who surrounded them. Neither my mother nor grandparents ever did, but to some extent they didn't need to in order to maintain their life situations. So what about me? How did I begin later to unlearn my racism? Was there a process?

Let's start with my having been mindless about matters of race and prejudice. Yes, I'd gone out with my Kansas City high school buddies to "throw some eggs at niggers," but that was a part of fitting in with the "in crowd," of being popular, and of peer approval. Race was insignificant in my life.

For example, the summer after high school I played semi-pro baseball around Kansas City, both in Missouri and Kansas, including games at the Federal Prison at Leavenworth, and at the State Prison at Lansing. Memories of those baseball days are readily accessible.

I can visualize our arriving at the prisons, and joking in an adolescent fashion about the prison atmosphere ("will they let us out if we win?"). I recall the classroom we dressed in due to their being no provisions for visitors to change their clothes. I recall how we were always accompanied by a staff member, how we walked onto manicured baseball fields and gazed up at armed guards atop each prison baseball park's right field wall. I can even remember a base hit I banged off a fifty-foot-tall brick wall at Leavenworth and seeing the right fielder play the carom off the bricks that he knew well—very well—from playing so many games on a single prison field.

But I have no memory of black ballplayers on the prison teams.

Years later, through the Society for American Baseball Research (SABR) I learned there were, indeed, black players on those prison teams. What's remarkable is not the fact that there were African American players, but that I didn't remember—because it wasn't important to me. I didn't care. I didn't care about race relations, about segregation, about prejudice, nor social injustice. Nor did I have to care. It just didn't come up.

Later, as a college student (1953-1957), I was a big fish in a small pond at what was then Emporia State Teachers College: leading actor, baseball player, and student council president. In 2003, I had to look at the college yearbook to determine whether there were any black students in my college! My yearbooks, *The Sunflower*, reveal there were, during my junior and senior years, at least two dozen students of color, some African Americans, some Pacific Islanders, and some Asian Americans, but because they hadn't been important to me I didn't remember them. That's how little attention I paid.

I'd married after my freshman year and my wife, Jackie, worked in the Registrar's Office with a Korean student, so we learned from him about Korean food, but I had no interest in his experience of racial difference in the small Kansas community. And the summer after my junior year, I painted the college stadium's seats with Danny Horouchi, a Hawaiian American football linebacker. On those steaming August days, I learned about Danny's family, about Honolulu and about Hawaii, and about how he was recruited. But I didn't have enough curiosity to ask about his experience of race and racism in college, in Emporia or, for that matter, in Honolulu.

Then I graduated and went off to teach in Kansas City schools five years after the Supreme Court had ruled in Brown v Board of Education in Topeka, Kansas, that "separate but equal" was not equal. Yet they still had no black students. I have no memory of asking, "Why? Why are there no black students in this school?" The school systems I taught for had dug in their heels against forced integration. They weren't going to give in without court fights; in fact, the Kansas City, MO, schools were released from court-ordered integration only in 1999. But I wasn't even curious. I was going along mindlessly in that part of my life, ignoring the racism that was embedded in my community. I wasn't getting my corn-pone from people of color, so they had no effect on my opinions nor were there people around me engaged in the struggle for civil rights.

In 1958, the U.S. was still maintaining a military draft. In those Cold War times, married men with children were regularly deferred from the draft, and teachers were also eligible for deferment. Jackie and I had postponed having children, and my draft board had a reputation for seldom deferring teachers, so with the Army hot on my heels, I tested my way into Navy Officer Candidate School for a three-year hitch. Then I found a way to reduce that commitment to two years as an enlisted man serving in Washington, DC, as part of the Navy's Ceremonial Guard, whose job was to bury veterans at Arlington National Cemetery.

On those funeral details, I helped carry the casket, and occasionally handed the flag to the widow who, almost on cue, dissolved in tears when "Taps" sounded. Several years later, just about every detail of President Kennedy's 1963 funeral was familiar to me: the riderless horse, the riflemen's firing, the folding of the American flag, even the bugle player's single off-key note occasioned by having to play "Taps" in the bone-chilling cold of Arlington Cemetery with the wind coming off the nearby Potomac River.

In addition to performing this solemn task, the nearly two years I served in the Navy was, to put it bluntly, my introduction to black people. I can't remember having a single conversation with a black person before entering the Navy at age twenty-three, and my eyes were truly opened.

At the Great Lakes Naval Training Station's "boot camp" north of Chicago, I was designated to serve as recruit company commander, and therefore, for the first time interacted daily with the half dozen black men in my company. At the time, I was totally ignorant of the historic importance of President Truman's having integrated the American military services only a decade or so before. But I remember being surprised that our small complement of black men was interesting, funny, and likeable. I remember the last week of boot camp, one of the black men, a short, handsome, and good-humored fellow, got into a barracks fistfight with a chubby white sailor from South Carolina. When I stepped in to break it up, the black fellow, maybe three inches shorter and forty pounds lighter than the Carolinian, stepped back and yelled at the Southerner, "Alright, motha fucka, just remember, you gotta go south—that's through Chicago—to get home. I'll be waiting." In an effort to avoid showing partisanship, I suppressed my laughter and my appreciation for his quick-witted linguistic facility, but I've treasured the moment ever since.

The U.S. Naval Receiving Station, located along the Anacostia River, had a black physician who treated me twice. I'd never encountered a black professional, and I remember finding it remarkable—a black physician! Our Ceremonial Guard unit had only one or two black men; one was Evans (I can't for the life of me remember his first name—we enlisted men were known by our last names). He stood about six-one or six-two, lean, handsome, private, and taciturn. I soon learned we had something in common: he had a theatre degree.

Evans was one of four men in the unit that I sought out for conversation. I was fascinated when I learned that he'd gone to Boston College, well known as a theatre school in one of America's leading theatre cities, while I was a graduate of a little teachers college in Emporia, Kansas, hardly the Athens of the Midwest. Years later I realized that our college had a remarkable group of student actors, a few of whom were admitted to England's Royal Academy of Dramatic Art, and several of us went on to successful careers as actors, directors and teachers. But at the time, Evans's having studied acting at Boston College impressed me. I was considering graduate studies—either actor training or a PhD program—so his thoughts about training interested me.

Around the same time, I was reading the great liberal defense attorney Clarence Darrow's autobiography, *The Story of My Life*, which was my memorable introduction to issues of social conscience and racial discrimination. While Darrow is perhaps most famous today for his involvement in the Scopes "Monkey Trial," I was more impressed that he had worked in defense of a black physician, Dr. Ossian Sweet, who had protected himself and his family when they were violently attacked in their newly purchased Detroit home in a white neighborhood. How naïve was I? I'd had no notion that a black physician, educated, respectable, and prosperous, was not welcome to live in a white neighborhood. I grew up thinking black people lived in separate neighborhoods because they wanted to.

After occasional conversations with Evans about acting and actor training, I inquired about his family and his background, and learned that his parents owned and operated a lumberyard in the Boston area and they had a suburban home near Boston. It may be that this was literally my introduction to the fact that there were black businessmen. I inquired about his family's experience of housing discrimination. He responded. "My parents have lived in our home all my life. It's an integrated neighborhood." Thinking of Dr. Sweet, I asked, "Do they have trouble with their neighbors?"

I have to wonder what he thought of my ignorance. "No. In fact, my mom and dad are happy with our neighborhood just the way it is." He grinned briefly. "Some Sunday mornings, Mother tells my dad to go out and work in the yard to scare away the white folks who're driving around looking for houses. She doesn't want to see the neighborhood change!"

I exaggerate only a bit when I say that I was in the process of learning that it wasn't true that all black people lived in slums or were Southern sharecroppers—a step toward un-learning my racism.

Over the eighteen months I spent in the Ceremonial Guard, Evans and I had only a dozen or so conversations—I lived off base with Jackie, while he lived in the barracks. After about nine months of burying people, shining shoes, polishing brass, and folding flags for tearful widows, I passed the Navy's test to become a Journalist Third Class, and began editing the base's newspaper. One out of four nights I had to spend my "duty night" as part of the base's security unit, policing gate traffic, checking on building security, and posting guards at parking lots. One of those nights, Evans and I talked about segregation, which he'd observed in parts of Boston but said he hadn't dealt with directly. I asked about restaurants, remarking that in my native Kansas City, restaurants were segregated.

"When I drive home to Boston to visit my parents," he told me, "there's a roadside restaurant, sort of a diner, in Maryland that I stop at, walk into, and stand at the counter. I make sure I'm well-dressed when I'm in civilian clothes, or sometimes I'll drive wearing my uniform. Waitresses notice but ignore me; finally one will give up and walk over to me and almost whisper, 'I'm sorry; we can't serve you.' I look her in the eye and say, 'I know, but I just wanted to embarrass you and your manager. After all, I'm a citizen and I'm serving in the Navy on active duty in Washington, DC.' I can see they're embarrassed and don't know what to say or do. Then I turn and walk out, get in my car and drive away. I do it every time I go to Boston or New York," he concluded. "I do it on every trip. It's what I can do." This certainly made an impression on me.

In 1959 and 1960, while Evans and I were serving together, North Carolina lunch counter sit-ins were capturing press and television attention. States and counties throughout the South wrestled with "forced integration" in various ways. For instance, Prince Edward County, Virginia, closed its public schools in 1959 while I was living north of there in the Washington DC, suburb of Arlington. Southern governors and senators warned of the mongrelizing of the races that would inevitably follow forced integration.

As I try, years after the fact, to reconstruct my process of unlearning racism, it feels profoundly important that I was in our nation's capital from January 1959 to June 1960. Race and the Cold War were often in the news. Armed Federal troops had been sent to integrate Little Rock schools in 1957; busses and trains here and there across America were being desegregated; racial issues were being argued in the House and in the Senate; filibusters by Southern politicians were still defeating antilynching laws. And for the first time in my life, I was reading a great daily newspaper, *The Washington Post.*

On a more personal level, my drive to work from our apartment in Arlington took me into the Anacostia section of Washington, presenting me daily with evidence of black unemployment and poverty. And I began to question whether the United States had a right to criticize other nations' treatment of their citizens when we were surrounded by such obvious discrimination against our own: in schools, housing (both urban and rural), education, and employment we treated African Americans as being less-than-equal to whites.

The sheer newness—the unfamiliarity—of Washington in 1959 impacted Jackie and me profoundly. Living a thousand miles from family and familiar sources of corn-pone, she and I saw the world with fresh eyes. We had lived in segregated Kansas City, but Washington and suburban Virginia, where we lived, was different from what we'd experienced, and one sometimes sees more perceptively that which one isn't accustomed to.

Washington was, in its way in the 'fifties, a Southern city with Southern manners and customs and with Southern segregation; but in other ways it was more integrated than the cities we had known. More than we ever had in the Midwest, we shopped alongside black people in downtown DC—a few of them poor and uneducated, but some of them well dressed and well educated, and that in itself was a new experience. Daily we traveled among more black people than we might have seen in a month or more in Kansas City; yes, there was obvious black poverty, but there was also a black middle class and a university, Howard University, that was considered the black Harvard. It was all so new!

The conversations with Evans led me to begin questioning long-held beliefs about black people—about their family structures, about their education (after all, Evans, a black man, had a more sophisticated understanding of theatre than mine). Reading Clarence Darrow, an old-fashioned union supporter, a "defender of the damned," an advocate for poor people, and an advocate for black people, led me to question my social and political beliefs.

In my first presidential vote in 1956, I'd supported Dwight Eisenhower, a moderately conservative Republican and a fellow Kansan. By the time Jackie and I left Washington in June 1960, I was a dedicated liberal who intended to vote for John F. Kennedy.

In an eighteen-month period, I'd arrived at new opinions about almost all aspects of American social and political life. I'd changed from being an uninformed racist who tacitly believed in the rightness of white supremacy, to being a person who was convinced that America had historically mistreated, and continued to mistreat its black citizens, and who believed we must begin immediately to reverse our pervasive patterns of racial discrimination. In fact, the racial, social, economic, and political beliefs I developed in those eighteen months in Washington are the convictions I've carried, deepening some and modifying others, ever since.

I'd determined that my social and political corn-pone had to come from people who understood and shared my conviction that three hundred years of American racial discrimination could no longer stand. There had to be change, and clearly change had to be forced upon those who intended to hang on to the social, political, and economic advantages that had been achieved through more than two hundred years of racial discrimination.

In addition to having my eyes opened concerning injustice in the U.S., it was during those years in the Navy that I made some of the most important decisions concerning my future. Should I pursue actor-training? I'd been encouraged by my undergraduate mentor, Karl Bruder, to think about going to New York to train and to pursue a professional acting career. I also saw that law school and the attorney's life was a realistic alternative. Or I could choose what I did: the theatre professor's career, studying history and theory.

I'd taught high school theatre and realized that I'd essentially read nothing and knew nothing, but I was confident I could learn. I chose the academic life: I loved learning, I had little interest in competing to be in a Broadway show where I'd do the same thing night after night, performance after performance, and I saw that many of the people I wanted to be with and wanted to be like were in the academic world. After all, they were admired for their knowledge; they enjoyed a varied life of learning and sharing; they had economic security (I learned later, of course, that you had to do something significant like writing scholarly articles to earn tenure.); and I had learned, somehow, that academics were freer to say what they thought than others, an especially important issue in the Cold War 'fifties.

Of course, in those times, Americans hesitated to criticize our country. In hindsight, I see clearly that McCarthyism had intimidated my teachers at Emporia State, intimidated the local and national press, and essentially intimidated the nation. Criticism of national policy implied to many that one was disloyal. Indeed, they were times in which loyalty was questioned; as a new graduate assistant at the University of Illinois, in June 1960, I had to sign a loyalty oath.

"Is it legal for you to require me to sign this just to go to school?" I didn't think it was legal, but I asked.

"You don't have to sign it in order to enroll in school," came the reply, "but Illinois law requires that all newly-hired State employees sign it." In other words, I had to sign it, even though I found it inappropriate and probably unconstitutional, if I were to collect my graduate assistantship stipend. With a three-months pregnant wife and no health insurance, I needed the assistantship's stipend and benefits. I signed—reluctantly—but I signed.

It embarrasses me today. I've sometimes thought I should have had the fortitude to confront this stupid law. I felt at the time there was no alternative, but I still detest the thought of having knuckled under to what I considered then and believe now to be an inappropriate and unconstitutional law. Later, when I read of demonstrations in the South, and when I saw reports of violence toward protesters, I thought often of Evans and his Delaware roadside restaurant, and his quietly doing what he could do. I admired his courageousness. It was getting more and more difficult for me to see race and racism as not part of my life.

For three years, Jackie and I lived in former World War II military barracks on campus. They were, to say the least, ramshackle and leaky, and rodent infested. After all, they had been built during World War II as temporary housing. We once saw a broken pipe's water flow across our kitchen and out, nothing slowing it, let alone stopping it, at a floorboard's half-inch opening across the room. On home-game Saturdays, trainloads of Illini football fans from Chicago and Cook County suburbs disembarked a few yards from our apartment and walked a pathway past our windows on their way to the stadium. I once heard a couple of women in their thirties ask, "Do you think people really live in these places?" But the rent was cheap, and we knew it was temporary; indeed, the buildings were demolished less than two years after I finished my degree.

For the last year and a half that we lived in the student housing, a black couple in their mid-twenties, Walt and Estelle and their baby, lived across the hall. Walt graduated in Electrical Engineering and accepted a West Coast aircraft industry job. Walt, Estelle, and their six-month-old baby girl were leaving in June, before Jackie's and my scheduled August departure. One spring evening, Walt and I stood talking on our shared front stoop.

"When will you leave for the job?" I asked him.

"In about ten days," he replied.

"Are they flying you to California?"

"They offered, but I want to keep the car, and they won't ship it, so we'll drive."

Surprised, I responded, "It's a three-day drive, any way you cut it, and maybe more because of the baby."

I didn't see him hesitate about his answer, "I've done a lot of phoning, and talking with people along the way. I've made sure we have a place to stay for four nights. We're taking four days to drive."

I started to say that it seemed a bit compulsive to plan each motel like that, but I caught myself. Walt saw that I understood, adding, "You can't take a baby across the country like that without knowing there's going to be a motel that will take you." This newly-minted electrical engineering graduate, a husband and father, couldn't be sure he could drive from Illinois, the Land of Lincoln, to Southern California and easily find overnight accommodations for his family.

It's a reality I've never personally had to face, and that conversation seared some very unpleasant realizations into my consciousness: to be a black person in the United States of America required then, and still requires, levels of awareness that no white person can fully appreciate. Walt and Estelle weren't traveling into the "deep South" that Freedom Riders and Martin Luther King and young black college students were integrating. They were driving from the Midwest to the Southwest of the United States, but they couldn't make the assumptions that Jackie and I took for granted with our two little ones. As white people we'd never had to think about the level of hostility that could face Walt and Estelle at any corner they might turn, anywhere in the United States.

When Evamarii talks to me now of "white privilege," that is what she's referring to: as white men and women, we have been awarded a lifetime privilege that we're not even aware of; we've been permitted the assumption that we can go anywhere we choose, when we choose, without being challenged for being who we are. Of course, today we have laws that theoretically prohibit discrimination of the sort Walt knew he might encounter, but those laws cannot preclude acts of discrimination that every black person knows he or she might encounter at the next turn.

For the doubter, I'll present two travel incidents in which Evamarii and I were driving separate cars across the country in 1991 and 1992. We were living in Evanston, Illinois, after I'd taken early retirement from Illinois State University, and we'd accepted temporary teaching at the California Institute of the Arts, a few miles northeast of Los Angeles—nearly the same drive that Walt made 25 years earlier. My parents were in their nursing home and no longer drove, so we took both their car and ours to California. Driving in Nevada, just east of the California border near Lake Tahoe, I was leading by a few car lengths when I looked in my rearview mirror and saw a Nevada Highway Patrol car pull Evamarii over. It took me fifty yards or more to stop safely and start walking back to where she and the patrolman were parked. By the time I was twenty yards away, he was headed back to his patrol car, and the "stop" was completed.

"What happened? Why'd he stop you?" Evamarii has a sense of irony: "He said I was driving inconsistently. He wanted to see my license and registration. When I looked toward you and said, 'My husband will know where the registration is,' he lost interest."

As soon as he saw the "husband" was a white guy, that Nevada Highway Patrolman was cruising his way down the road and away from us, with neither explanation nor excuse. He'd stopped a middle-aged black woman, apparently concerned that she was "driving while black," a common offense on American roads, more common than most white folks are aware of or willing to acknowledge.

The very next year, 1992, we were driving the same two cars, this time east from LA after another semester teaching at the California Institute of the Arts, headed toward the

California/Nevada border; we'd agreed to reconnoiter for a rest stop outside Barstow, California. Evamarii was so unusually late that I worried for a few minutes in the heat until she arrived, hot and angry, and explained that the delay was occasioned by a California Highway Patrol officer who stopped her, once more for a driving pattern he'd observed: "You seemed to be pulling to the right." A middle-aged African American woman driving a nondescript seven-year-old brown Toyota Celica was pulled over once again, apparently for "driving while black." And, to cap the matter, she told me, "If that Toyota pulls at all, it pulls left!"

And so I am reminded, as a white man, that racism continues to exist in America, and continues to have an impact on the daily lives of African Americans in this country. It is too easy for the lens of white privilege to allow one to slip back into complacency concerning matters of race.

Chapter 4

Taking a Stand

"I am an anti-imperialist. I am opposed to having the eagle put its talons on any other land."
– Mark Twain in the *New York Herald* (1900)

"We are of the Anglo-Saxon race, and when the Anglo-Saxon wants a thing he just takes it."
– Chairman of the Ends of the Earth Club (1906)

In 1895, as part of his effort to lift his family out of debt and restore them to dignity, Twain began a round-the-world lecture tour that took him, Livy, and daughter Clara across the upper tier of American states, to Vancouver, BC, then to Australia, New Zealand, Ceylon, India, and South Africa before they sailed to England where they settled, intending to stay there while Twain composed his book about the voyage, *Following the Equator*. But soon after they had settled in London, word came that their eldest daughter, Susy, was ill; Livy sailed immediately for the U.S., while Twain stayed in London. Before Livy could reach her, Susy died of spinal meningitis. The family, bereft, began a lengthy period of mourning, limiting their contact with outsiders, while Twain worked, literally day and night, on the travel book.

Following the Equator by no means focuses primarily on race, but some of its most energetic and compelling passages deal with white men's brutality toward aboriginal people around the world. For example, he describes white settlers in Queensland, Australia, who weren't used to "savages":

They could not understand the primary law of savage life: that if a man do you a wrong, his whole tribe is responsible—each individual of it—and you may take your change out of any individual of it, without bothering to seek out the guilty one. When a white killed an aboriginal, the tribe applied the ancient law, and killed the first white man they came across. To the whites this was a monstrous thing. Extermination seemed to be the proper medicine for such creatures as this. They did not kill all the blacks, but they promptly killed enough of them to make their own persons safe. From the dawn of civilization down to this day the white man has always used that very precaution.[17]

And, after telling of Queensland whites that murdered a whole aboriginal tribe, he demands that we realize these brutalities are not limited to a single place.

In many countries we have chained the savage and starved him to death; and this we do not care for, because custom has inured us to it; yet a quick death by poison is lovingkindness to it. In many countries we have burned the savage at the stake; and this we do not care for, because custom has inured us to it; yet a quick death is lovingkindness to it. In more than one country we have hunted the savage and his little children and their mother with dogs and guns through the woods and swamps for an afternoon's sport, and filled the region with happy laughter over their sprawling and stumbling flight, and their wild supplications for mercy; but this method we do not mind because custom has inured us to it; yet a quick death by poison is lovingkindness to it. In many countries we have taken the savage's land from him, and made him our slave, and lashed him every day, and broken his pride, and made death his only friend, and overworked him till he dropped in his tracks; and this we do not care for, because custom has inured us to it; yet a quick death by poison is lovingkindness to it. In the Matabeleland to-day—why, there we are confining ourselves to sanctified custom, we Rhodes-Beit millionaires in South Africa and Dukes in London; and nobody cares, because we are used to the old holy customs, and all we ask is that no notice-inviting new ones shall be intruded upon the attention of our comfortable consciences.[18]

One can argue that this is as close as Mark Twain came, in his published work after 1876, to confronting the cruelties of post-Civil War racial violence as practiced in his own country. Yes, he cites violence from many countries—notably South Africa and England, in addition to Australia, while never directly addressing racial violence in the United States—but clearly the examples were recognizable to American readers.

Twain, in *Following the Equator*, wrote as directly as he ever had about his personal experience of slavery and white brutality toward black people. He eases casually into the topic, describing the unforgettable experience of his arriving with his family in India where, "Even now, after the lapse of a year, the delirium of those days in Bombay has not left me, and I hope it never will. It was all so new, no detail of it hackneyed."[19] A burly German, accompanied by three natives, accompanied him to the family's rooms, followed by fourteen additional native servants, each of whom carried a single article (a coat, a book, a fan); each waited for a tip, shyly expressed his gratitude, and went away. He describes them as soft and gentle, both winning and touching. Something on a balcony door needed cleaning, so one native got on his knees and began to work; the man seemed to be doing the job adequately, but the German, without comment, gave the native a cuff on the jaw and then pointed out the problem.

I had not seen the like of this for fifty years. It carried me back to my boyhood, and flashed upon me the forgotten fact that this was the usual way of explaining one's desires to a slave. I was able to remember that the method seemed right and natural to me in those days, I being born to it and unaware that elsewhere there were other methods; but I was also able to remember that those unresented cuffings made me sorry for the victim and ashamed for the punisher. My father was a refined and kindly gentleman, very grave, rather austere, of rigid probity, a sternly just and upright man, albeit he attended no church and never spoke of religious matters, and had no part nor lot in the pious joys of his Presbyterian family, nor ever seemed to suffer from this deprivation. He laid his hand upon me in punishment only twice in his life, and then not heavily; once for telling him a lie—which surprised me, and showed me how unsuspicious he was, for that was not my maiden effort. He punished me those two times only and never any other member of the family at all; yet every now and then he cuffed our harmless slave boy, Lewis, for trifling little blunders and awkwardnesses. My father had passed his life among the slaves from his cradle up, and his cuffings proceeded from the custom of the time, not from his nature. When I was ten years old I saw a man fling a lump of iron-ore at a slave-man in anger, for merely doing something awkwardly—as if that were a crime. It bounded from the man's skull, and the man fell and never spoke again. He was dead in an hour. I knew the man had a right to kill his slave if he wanted to, and yet it seemed a pitiful thing and somehow wrong, though why wrong I was not deep enough to explain if I had been asked to do it. Nobody in the village approved of that murder, but of course no one said much about it.[20]

It is notable that Mark Twain introduces these vivid descriptions of white violence toward colored servants and slaves quietly, unobtrusively. Perhaps he was homing in on a fine line that he knew he must not cross, a line that if he stood behind allowed him to describe his personal experience of white brutality toward black people while subtly protecting himself from accusation that he was criticizing his fellow white Americans back home who were engaging in acts of violence toward black people.

An argument can be made that his trip around the world put race in a new light for him; as a result of his travels, especially to Australia and New Zealand, he saw that the mistreatment of colored people by white people was an international sickness. If he couldn't write directly about American problems, he could at least point to comparable abuses around the world, perhaps inspiring American readers to look inward at their country's treatment of its black citizens.

Later, while he was still in Vienna, Twain learned of America's deepening confrontation against Spain in Cuba. At first he approved, believing it to be a righteous mission intended to free people whom Spain had held captive. Twain wrote his minister friend, Joe Twichell, whose son had volunteered for service, that he approved of the war because it was being fought for another people's freedom, "and I think this is the first time it has been done."[21]

However, the United States went on to occupy Puerto Rico, Guam, and the Philippines, leading Twain to reconsider his support of America's adventure in imperialism. By the time he returned to the States in fall of 1900, after a decade of living mostly abroad, he was lionized for having accomplished the nearly unprecedented feat of repaying his and his wife's debts. He may have been, by then, the most famous American, and perhaps the most famous private person in the world. The press wanted to ask him about everything: manners, policemen, cabs, fashions, theatres; as Ron Powers says, "America had missed him. America had found something missing in itself when he was away, it almost seemed."[22]

The questions at the dock came 'round to America's military adventures abroad, and Twain declared himself unequivocally:

I left these shores, at Vancouver, a red-hot imperialist. I wanted the American eagle to go screaming into the Pacific. It seemed tiresome and tame for it to content itself with the Rockies. Why not spread its wings over the Philippines, I asked myself? And I thought it would be a real good thing to do.

I said to myself, here are a people who have suffered for three centuries. We can make them as free as ourselves, give them a government and country of their own, put a miniature of the American constitution afloat in the Pacific, start a brand new republic to take its place among the free nations of the world. It seemed to me a great task to which we had addressed ourselves.

But I have thought some more, since then, and I have read carefully the treaty of Paris, and I have seen that we do not intend to free, but to subjugate the people of the Philippines. We have gone there to conquer, not to redeem.

We have also pledged the power of this country to maintain and protect the abominable system established in the Philippines by the Friars.

It should, it seems to me, be our pleasure and duty to make those people free, and let them deal with their own domestic questions in their own way. And so I am an anti-imperialist. I am opposed to having the eagle put its talons on any other land.[23]

From 1901 on, Twain was one of America's leading anti-imperialists; so, of course, he incurred the scorn that comes almost inevitably to one who speaks against a wartime majority.[24]

Twain didn't, though, limit himself to criticizing American leaders and their foreign policies. He joined in criticism of King Leopold of Belgium who had engaged for years in brutalizing Congo's natives. One of his most effective political writings was "King Leopold's Soliloquy," an essay that was rejected by his publishers at Harper & Brothers, although they allowed him to give it away, free of royalty, to a Congo reform group. But, for whatever reasons, he didn't choose to stay long with the issue of Leopold's atrocities in the Congo. Justin Kaplan, in his Pulitzer Prize and National Book Award-winning biography, *Mr. Clemens and Mark Twain*, quotes Twain: "My instincts and interests are merely literary, they rise no higher; and I scatter from one interest to another, lingering nowhere."[25]

It may be that we should take Twain at his word and accept him as having the impulse he asserts: to scatter from one interest to another. But what are we to make of his regular return, from 1874 on, to the subject of race and white men's mistreatment of black people around the world? What are we to make of *Adventures of Huckleberry Finn*'s and *Pudd'nhead Wilson*'s explorations of satire, irony and metaphor in treating racial injustices? What are we to make of his 1901 effort to get Harper and Brothers to publish his essay, "The United States of Lyncherdom"? Justin Kaplan estimates that during the 1890s, over one thousand five hundred lynchings took place; in 1901 alone there were 130. That same year, in Twain's native Missouri, there was a much-publicized lynching of three men in the southwest corner of the state. That summer Twain wrote in white-hot passion, pleading for American missionaries in China to return to America where they were needed in the lynching fields of Missouri. If they were brave enough to face "heathen" Chinese, he argued, they were brave enough to "come home and convert these Christians."[26] He proposed "The United States of Lyncherdom" to Frank Bliss as part of a book project, a history of lynching. But within days, he acknowledged the corn-pone realities: it would be disastrous for him in the South, killing his book sales, "I shouldn't have even half a friend left down there after it issued from the press."[27]

Could there be a more corn-pone opinion? The "Lyncherdom" essay made clear how Mark Twain felt about white mistreatment of black people. But his letter to Bliss made equally clear that getting his corn-pone was more important than having the world know how much he hated racial abuses.

*****

The major difference between Twain's unlearning racism and mine is that we got our corn-pone in different places and at different times.

My unlearning was easy compared to his: after growing up a racist, I entered adulthood at just the right time. World War II newsreels had shown us death camps and bones and bodies and gas chambers, and Americans were starting to realize that we couldn't criticize the Soviets for denying freedom to their people and to Eastern Europe unless we quit discriminating in the North and abandoned Jim Crow abuses in the South. When the Navy sent me to Washington in 1959, I changed my corn-pone sources just as America was gaining steam and ready to explode into the 1960s and the Civil Rights revolution.

As easy as it was for me, it was that much more difficult for Twain to publicly express his opposition to Jim Crow. As a young man, he'd barely begun unlearning his racism when America abandoned our freed slaves and left them to their own devices. Soon after Twain put his toe in the waters of anti-racism with "A True Story," the United States of America turned its blind eye toward its former slaves; it abandoned them in 1877 to racial discrimination and violence. Over the next thirty-five years or so of Twain's life, white men increasingly arrogated to themselves privilege and superiority based on race. Like a slow-starting but soon fast-moving steam locomotive, the South passed law after law that required segregation, discouraged black voting and threw a blanket of discrimination over the region. And the courts confirmed one after another of those Jim Crow laws.

At the same time the South was imposing brutal restrictions on Southern black citizens, Northern opposition to extreme racism was dissipating. C. Vann Woodward, in his seminal book, *The Strange Career of Jim Crow*, blames the rest of America for tolerating Southern abuses. "All the elements of fear, jealousy, proscription, hatred and fanaticism," he writes, "had long been present, as they are present in various degrees of intensity in any society. What enabled them to rise to dominance . . . was a general weakening and discrediting of the numerous forces that had hitherto kept them in check."[28] To illustrate Northern complicity Woodward quotes a South Carolina senator who, in 1900, thanked a Massachusetts colleague, "for his complete announcement of the divine right of the Caucasian to govern the inferior races"; for the South Carolinian this was a complete vindication of his state and region's practices.[29]

For us at the beginning of the twenty-first Century, it is hard to imagine how unapologetic the American people and its leadership had become in their white superiority as they oversaw the destruction of Native Americans in the West, and the imperialist conquest of Cuba and the Philippines. In 1906 Twain, still an anti-imperialist, wrote (but not for publication) that, "At the banquet last winter of that organization which calls itself the Ends of the Earth Club, the chairman, a retired regular army officer of high grade, proclaimed in a loud voice, and with fervency, 'We are of the Anglo-Saxon race, and when the Anglo-Saxon wants a thing he just takes it.'"[30] Living in such a blatantly racist culture, it's no wonder that Twain—who we have every reason to believe sympathized with black Americans—abandoned his book about lynching. He was getting his corn-pone from an unapologetically racist culture, so it's no wonder that at he also abandoned a novel that explored reversing black/white power relations.[31]

*****

Mine was an easier path. I had only the two decades of my youth in which to learn my racism—only a few years to learn and adopt the privileges of American white superiority. Ironically, in the 1940s and 1950s I started learning to be a racist at the same time America was, however fitfully, reversing its course, heading in the other direction. In the same years Grandpa Pritner regaled me with jokes about Rastus and his friend eating puke – in those very years Major League Baseball was being integrated by Jackie Robinson, Larry Doby, Roy Campanella, Don Newcombe, Satchel Paige, and a host of other Negro League players. The Dixiecrats were splitting from the Democratic Party over Southern insistence on white supremacy, and Harry Truman was signing executive orders against discrimination in the military and in Federal hiring.

During my college years there were racial events I could have paid attention to but didn't: in 1954 the Supreme Court decided that "separate but equal" hadn't worked in American schools; in 1955 Rosa Parks went to jail for refusing to sit where white folks wanted her to sit on a Montgomery, Alabama, bus; in the same year, Congress decided that interstate busses and trains had to be integrated; and in 1957 Arkansas used its National Guard to fight against integrating its schools. All of these were events I could have made important in my life – but I don't remember doing so. What little social awareness I had in the 1940s and 1950s was much more focused on anti-

Communism, the Red Scare, right-wing radio, McCarthyism, and Grandpa Pritner's right-wing politics.

One 1948 example symbolizes for me the overwhelmingly conservative atmosphere I grew up in. All of Hartford's indoor events of consequence transpired in "the school auditorium." It was a one-building school—kindergarten through twelfth grades, all in one building, and with a single auditorium that accommodated study halls in the daytime, school entertainments at night, movies, lectures, and political gatherings. On a memorable winter evening, the auditorium was packed with 150 students and adults—remember, we're talking about a Kansas town of less than five hundred—for a lecture sponsored by the American Medical Association, whose purpose was to warn us of the Soviet Communist intent to take over American medicine. "The world's finest medical system," according to the lecturer, was threatened by Socialized Medicine, the kind of medicine that England, that very year, was putting into operation. Under this Communist-inspired system we would, he said, no longer have a choice of doctors and hospitals; and most importantly, the system of "Socialized Medicine" was merely a foot in the door. If America were to make the mistake of accepting Socialized Medicine, it would be a major step toward our nation being dominated by International Communism. No adult in the audience objected. None questioned a word that was spoken that night. I heard and believed that story for the next ten years.

It's no wonder my first presidential vote was for Dwight David Eisenhower, a native Kansan, a gradualist on race and integration who, while the decisive school integration case was being decided, took the Chief Justice of the Supreme Court,

Earl Warren, by the arm and said of Southern segregationists, "These are not bad people. All they are concerned about is to see that their sweet little girls are not required to sit in school alongside some big overgrown Negroes."[32]

Somehow—and I don't really know how—when I got to Washington in 1959, I was primed for social and political conversion. In less than a year and a half, I transformed myself. I shed a conservative skin, and began what has proven a life-long attachment to progressivism. Part of it was the visibility of Southern racism in the Washington, DC, and Northern Virginia area (the *Washington Post* fed me a near-daily diet of stories describing Southern Congressmen's opposition to civil rights legislation) and part of it was the poverty and unemployment I encountered daily in the Anacostia neighborhood surrounding my naval base. And frankly, I found myself abhorring the way military people I was encountering saw the world. So it was a mixture of new ideas through the media and new experiences in my day-to-day life that seems to have tipped the scale.

When I became the editor of the base newspaper with more time on my hands than work to do, I soon realized that the search for news was a license for freedom. I bird-dogged military bases in the DC area, where I heard stories about admirals retiring and going to work for the defense contractors they'd been buying equipment from. I asked questions and learned about military budgets. I sat in the gallery and heard the Senate debate a bill. I sat in on Congressional committee meetings. In the eighteen months I served in Washington, I met one officer, and only one—a US Navy Lieutenant for whom I worked in Special Services—who had what might be called a social conscience, who acknowledged that the military almost certainly wouldn't have integrated racially if it hadn't been forced. It would be an oversimplification to say the Navy turned me from a conservative into a liberal—but it was while I was in the Navy that I became one.

It is significant, however, that I have never suffered a penalty for my liberalism. At the same time that Evans was telling me about his home life and was describing the Maryland diner's refusal to seat him, I had superiors who were devoted conservatives, yet I never suffered for disagreeing with them. In graduate school, when I learned from Walt about his need to plan for each night's hotel as he drove his family from Illinois to California, I lived in a progressive environment and I never suffered for supporting black Americans' fight against discrimination.

Which is not to say that the late 1950s and early 1960s were easy times in which to become a social progressive, even on university campuses. In 1953, a professor at my undergraduate school was fired merely for signing a petition that appeared in a national newspaper; and that same year a professor at the University of Kansas City was fired for "failing to divulge biographical details to the university."[33] Just before I got to the University of Illinois, the FBI had visited the campus and asked my theatre professors, "Why are you performing plays by a Russian, this Anton Chekhov, and why are you performing *The Threepenny Opera* by an East German Communist, Bertolt Brecht?"

So I may not have suffered for my liberalism, but the aftermath of McCarthyism and witch-hunts continued into the 1960s. Remember the loyalty oath I signed?

My first professorial job offered even more progressive corn-pone. In 1964 the Southern Illinois University-Edwardsville theatre program was housed temporarily in the abandoned East St. Louis, Illinois, high school building. Trucks on Highway US 40 roared by, north and south of the old building, and the campus neighborhood was predominantly black. For the first time in my life I was teaching classes that had as many as one-fourth black students, and I enjoyed the mix.

In the faculty lounge of the former school cafeteria, I ate almost daily with my sociologist colleague, Elliott Rudwick, who fed my hunger to learn about the history of white on black violence in the East St. Louis race riot of 1917. I must have been open-mouthed in my surprise when he explained that the previous summer's Watts riot was an historical anomaly—most of the truly violent race riots in American history had involved predominantly white on black violence. He told me of race riots I'd known nothing about, ones that involved primarily white violence perpetrated on black people: Wilmington, North Carolina, in 1898; Atlanta, Georgia, in 1906; Springfield, Illinois, in 1908; Chicago in 1911, Tulsa in 1921, and one during my lifetime that I'd heard nothing about—Detroit during World War II in 1943. I recall vividly my shock when he described the Springfield, Tulsa, Chicago, and Detroit riots, and I remember thinking, "I don't remember being taught about any of this! I had a two-semester course in American history; why didn't this get taught?"

In my next faculty position, at Illinois State University, I was honored when my department chair asked if I'd be willing to serve on the Task Force on Inter-Group Relations. Art White had commanded a black infantry company in World War II; he cared about the welfare of black people in America; his nominating me was a mindful act. By doing so, he was saying, in effect, that it was my time to take a stand.

*****

I'd been a member of the administration-appointed Task Force on Inter-Group Relations since its creation in 1968. The task force offered an opportunity for a few white faculty and students to meet regularly with representative black students and black faculty. It was a forum for the expression of concerns, a place for representative students and faculty to begin a process of understanding each other.

Climbing the stairs of Stevenson Hall on the ISU campus, I carried a single-spaced yellow legal pad with a few notes: "demand: a peremptory request," "Malcom X had been a racist, but he changed; he died, in part, for being a humanist," "we're not deciding to name a building after him—we're urging that a request be considered."

The ISU Council, twenty elected faculty and administration representatives, was meeting in the campus's largest public meeting room. I was ten minutes early, but there were fewer than half a dozen empty seats. As I headed toward one of the vacant seats a Council member said, "There's a seat reserved for you. You're testifying." "Sure, thanks," I mumbled. Indeed, I (a really white, balding, bearded, untenured associate professor of theatre) was to testify on behalf of the Task Force on Intergroup Relations in support of the Black Students Association's "demand" that the student union be named for Malcolm X.

69

ISU sits on the blackest soil in the Midwest—maybe the blackest soil in America. The land surrounding the university is so rich it's dedicated to growing the most valuable corn in the US—hybrid seed corn—the seeds farmers use to plant their corn crops. But in 1969 most of the black people in McLean County, Illinois, were students at ISU, perhaps three hundred out of a student population of more than twelve thousand, or about one-fourth of one percent. In 1969 the ninety-nine (or so) percent white citizens of Bloomington and Normal were upset, and had been for months, by the number of black students the university had recruited.

To state the obvious, 1969 was a year of troubles on American college and university campuses. In addition to protests against an unpopular war in Vietnam, colleges and universities faced racial conflicts. ISU's black students, many of them recruited from Joliet, Chicago, and its suburbs, were upset that winter by what they experienced as being ghettoized on a white campus, and they were further angered by what they saw as the campus's passive, tolerant response to Chicago police having killed Mark Clark and Fred Hampton, two Black Panther leaders who had been rousted from sleep and shot.

Feeling that the University administration wasn't responding to their concerns, black students presented a series of demands. Yes, they called them demands at a time when white folks weren't accustomed to considering demands from black folks. The general public in Republican-voting McLean County, home to America's largest auto insurer, State Farm Insurance, were surprised and even angered by the ISU administration's having agreed to meet some of the black students' demands for representation on the campus radio station's and school newspaper's staffs. But naming the University Union for the late Malcolm X was unpopular even with many on the supposedly liberal university campus, and naming a building for a black activist was anathema to the off-campus community.

The university president, Sam Braden, a mature and humane man, didn't refuse the demand for naming the Union after Malcolm X. Instead, he asked that the Task Force review this specific demand and make a recommendation to the University Council. Charles Morris, a black professor of mathematics, like me a relatively new Ph.D. from nearby University of Illinois, Urbana, chaired the Task Force, which voted to tell the University Council that black people are best-suited to identify their community's heroes, and that therefore naming a building for Malcolm X was appropriate.

Charles called me at home the evening after the Task Force vote. He said, "Cal, I think you're the person who's most appropriate to present the Task Force's response to the Council."

Who knows how long I paused? I had to confess to him that even though I'd voted support, "I don't know as much as I should about Malcolm X."

Now Charles paused. He's a Southern Gentleman. Over subsequent years, I got to know him socially and played tennis with him and his wife; Charles can wait a long time in a pause. He out-waited me.

"You're sure you think it's best for me to do it?" I asked, hoping against hope that he'd change his mind.

Pause... "Yes."

I was too slow-witted to come up with an argument.

"OK," I said. "I may have to call you for some advice."

*****

I'd not read *The Autobiography of Malcolm X*, but in the time between Charles's call on the evening of January 6 and my going before the Council on January 21, 1970, and during preparations for four classes, and department business, and family, and fear, and worry and more fear, I read the *Autobiography*. Twice. Did I mention I was afraid? Of what? Well, I suspect, I was afraid of embarrassing myself. There's no reason to believe my fears were either idealistic or unselfish.

So I read the book. The most important discovery—the Voila! Moment—came when I realized that this man, whom frankly I had known only from the media's one-sided portrayals of him as a black Muslim militant, was a leader who'd been transformed by his Hajj visit and who, when he was assassinated in 1965, had recognized the need for black and white people to live together in peace. In fact, the *Autobiography of Malcolm X* introduced me to one of America's more brilliant social thinkers, and to a man of peace.

Having taken a seat near the Council's meeting area, I waited and listened. After the usual preliminaries (reading the minutes, etc.), the Council moved quickly to its major agenda item: the Task Force on Inter-Group Relations' recommendations, as per President Braden's request.

Professor Chuck Hicklin, Council Chair, invited me to the table and introduced me—literally introduced me because, after all, I was in only my third year on campus, and to most of these campus leaders I was a near-stranger.

After taking my seat, in a hall filled to standing room, with radio microphones dangling from poles held above the audience, and with reporters grasping pens perched above lined yellow pads, I felt my knees shake. Not uncontrollably, but shaking enough that I wondered whether it was noticeable. Then came a moment of insight born of desperation: I'd taught three years of high school and two years of college public speaking, and I'd given students simple advice about fear in public speaking situations—situational anxiety. "Stage fright's normal," I'd tell them. "The best way to handle it is to have something you really want to say to your audience. If what you're saying is important to you, and if you focus on the importance of the message rather than on yourself, the hands shaking and the knees knocking will go away. You'll probably forget within five minutes that you were scared when you started." It was good advice; I took it. I remember that better than I remember anything about that night—and about five minutes into my presentation I noticed my hands weren't shaking, and my kneecaps weren't rattling.

"The Task Force asked me to represent them here tonight, and it's my pleasure to do so," I began. I then read a brief statement reiterating the Task Force's conviction that black people, black students and faculty, should have the primary voice in identifying their community's heroes, and recommending that the Council accept that recommendation.

I asked, and was granted, the opportunity to make a couple of statements of my own. I took a breath.

In preparing to meet with you tonight, I tried to anticipate some of your questions. I figured one concern might relate to the Black Students Association having presented "demands." So, I looked in the biggest dictionary my wife and I own, and found that the first meaning of demand is: "A peremptory request." Peremptory I think has to do with urgency — importance. Let's face it; black Americans have been put off for over a hundred years. Their needs haven't always been thought of as being urgent or important. So, I think we can understand a "peremptory request." It's a matter of importance, an urgent matter.

The room was silent. I continued:

The other concern I anticipated has to do with Malcolm X. Maybe you've read the *Autobiography of Malcolm X*. Until a couple of weeks ago I hadn't; but since then I've read it a couple of times. I was surprised to learn of a man who wasn't the person I felt the media had presented to America. I learned that, yes, he carried anger and the impulse to violence from his adolescence into his young adult years. He hated white people for what they'd done to him and to his family and to his people. But, he was a man who changed. He transformed himself after he traveled to Mecca and participated in the Hajj. He turned, in his last years, from an unfocused hatred, to an intense quest for peace and justice for his people. By the time he was assassinated he had discovered a Muslim religious life that celebrated equality among all people, men and women, black and white. We might even say he was assassinated in part because of changes he'd made, changes in his heart, changes that resulted in his holding new and more peaceful beliefs.

The Task Force asks that you approve its recommendation: That President Braden propose to the Board of Regents that they, the Regents, name the Illinois State University Student Union for Malcolm X, a man who preached peace and love for all people, no matter their color.

Did the Council have questions? You bet! They asked, "Had the Task Force polled all black students?" "No, but the students told us there is a consensus in favor of naming for Malcolm X. The task force relied on an oral report from a meeting at which a majority of black students were present, and there was near unanimity."

Then there was a motion recommending further surveying black student opinion. It failed.

Another motion came; this one proposed that a building other than the Student Union be named for Malcolm X. That motion failed.

Finally, after the question was called, there was a twelve to eight vote to accept the Task Force's recommendation! There were cheers in the room, to which the Chair, Chuck Hicklin, responded with a request for decorum. I barely had access to decorum myself. I felt like Clarence Darrow after he'd won a case! I'd never imagined we'd win! Twenty white professors and administrators, several who'd been on this campus for decades, some of whom I knew weren't happy with the direction the University was taking, had voted to support the idea of naming the Student Union – in some ways the most visible building on campus other than the administration building—after a black hero, Malcolm X.

The meeting dismissed. Reporters gathered around. I have no memory of their specific questions, but I recall that they were curious as to where this would lead. Perhaps everyone in the room was, at least to some extent, amazed by the outcome.

A few days later the Student Union Board voted to support the Task Force recommendation. Three official groups – the Task Force, the University Council, and the Student Union Board – had voted to recommend the naming.

*****

But the euphoria didn't last.

President Braden had been out of town when the Council had met. He came to the next Task Force meeting and there he explained that, after days of consultation and consideration, he had decided to forward the groups' positive recommendations, but that he felt he had to tell the Board of Regents that he could not, in the best interests of the University, support naming the Student Union after such a controversial public figure as Malcolm X.

I immediately raised my hand, got Braden's permission to speak, and announced, "President Braden, by doing this you are committing a riot against democracy!" OK, "Riot against democracy" might have been just a bit over the top, but Braden kept his temper. He didn't even call me an immature show-off.

He acknowledged I was right in my vote count, but he added, "It is my responsibility to act in what I believe to be the best interests of the University."

Back in my campus office half an hour after the meeting, my phone rang. It was the President's secretary, "President Braden wants to speak with you." I figured my tenure was decided, and not in my favor. Why did I buy a house before getting promotion and tenure? Sam came on the line: "Cal, I'd like to come down to your office and talk for a few minutes. Can you stick around until five?"

"Sure. Yes."

"Thanks, I'll be there about five."

I hung up and called, my wife: "I just got a call from President Braden," I told her, trying to sound calm. "He's coming to my office about five o'clock. I hope I haven't screwed everything up. I don't think they can fire me for what I've done. Tenure me? I dunno." She was patient and understanding, but I suspect she was as scared as I was.

Sam Braden was probably fifty-five at the time, but he had hair as white as your white Crayola crayon from grade school. He was probably five-nine or five-ten and carried only a few extra pounds at the waist. If you looked in the Central Casting directory under "university president," he'd resemble the pictures there.

He knocked at my open door. I rose and offered him the only seat other than my desk chair, and then sat when he did, prepared to be taken to the woodshed. But his eyes were as kind

77

as his words were measured and specific. No exhibition of power or authority, no yelling, not even a sense of urgency, merely straight, calm talk. Sam spoke of academic freedom, describing his experience at Indiana University, telling me in detail how the principle of academic freedom was the firewall that enabled the university to protect sex researcher Alfred Kinsey's tenure, recalling his admiration for the university president's courage in defending Kinsey against a state full of legislators and laymen who couldn't understand or agree with protecting a man who wrote the way Kinsey had about sex.

Sam acknowledged that the campus votes were an expression of faculty and student attitudes, that the votes were important, but that he also believed the university would be better served by naming some other building after a black person of stature, and that he intended to see that happen. And it did, later.

In the fall, to my great relief, I was notified that I had been granted tenure and appointed chairperson of a newly created Department of Theatre. I'd taken a stand, and the principle of academic freedom had worked—I had disagreed publicly with the president of the university and had paid no penalty for it.

Do I wish today that the Illinois State University Student Union were named in honor of Malcolm X? Yes, because he deserved the honor. Because a building named in his honor would celebrate a time when questions were asked about American racial segregation and racial prejudice. Because a few of the tens of thousands of students who have attended the University since then might have asked, "Why is this student-centered building named in honor of a Black Muslim militant?"

In pursuing their answers, a few might have found themselves confronting issues of American social history. If there's anything we need from our college students, it's curiosity—the asking and answering of questions about important and complex issues upon which they may be asked to take a stand.

At a personal level, it was a major turning point. I'm not as important as Alfred Kinsey, nor as important as others who have been protected by the principles of intellectual freedom that prevail in academe, but I know that I survived taking a stand against the campus's equivalent of the CEO—the University's president. Would a third-year employee in any line of endeavor other than a university get away with accusing the boss of "rioting against democracy," and get promoted within months to lifetime tenure and appointment to a major leadership position? Not likely.

I had made the decision to earn a doctorate and to pursue a life in academia somewhat blindly. When I made the decision, I had almost no understanding of the American academy's systems of appointment, promotion and tenure. Initially I knew merely that I loved the theatre, loved its necessary system of collaboration among artists and technicians, loved the sense of engagement and excitement that I got from working for weeks and sometimes months on a play without certain knowledge of success or failure, loved the intellectual challenge of reading and interpreting complex texts — and then embodying them before an audience, and I loved the sense of danger that is central to live theatre's interaction between actors and audience. Being a theatre professor might satisfy all these hungers, while at the same time providing a place where one could pursue ideas through reading, and teaching, and interacting with people who shared my interests and my intellectual curiosities. And, not unimportantly, I could provide my family with a middle-class living.

What I didn't realize was that it would allow me the ability to speak truth to power with a modicum of safety, which was a luxury that Twain, nor many others who found themselves called on to risk their corn-pone to push back against injustice, didn't have.

Chapter 5

More Unlearning

"I am quite sure I have no race prejudices, and I think I have no color prejudices, nor caste prejudices nor creed prejudices. Indeed, I know it. I can stand any society. All that I care to know is that a man is a human being — that is enough for me; he can't be any worse."
– Mark Twain, "Concerning the Jews" (1899)

"It's all about 1876. You can't understand Twain and race in America if you don't understand 1876."
– Student to Calvin Pritner (1994)

In the fall of 1994, Evamarii and I were guest faculty at the California Institute of the Arts, a Disney-founded arts college just across I-5 from the Magic Mountain theme park northeast of LA. At intermission of a student theatre production, we were chatting with one of her acting students and his Southerner boyfriend when lobby lights signaled the interval's end. The boyfriend asked, "What are you doing besides teaching actors about Shakespeare and his times?"

"A couple of years ago I got started reading Mark Twain — stuff he wrote, and books about him — and it's become a passion. I'm reading his last travel book, *Following the Equator*. He fascinates me as a Southerner. He was way ahead of his time — racism was all around him, North and South, but somehow he taught himself to be less of a racist than most folks. I've read *Huckleberry Finn* a couple of times, but now I have to reread it just for what I can figure out about Twain and race."

As we parted company at the theatre's entrance, the Southerner called out from ten feet away, "It's all about 1876. You can't understand Twain and race and America if you don't understand 1876."

What did he mean? We never saw him again, so I won't know for certain. But I've come to believe he was referring to the U.S. Presidential election of 1876, the election's aftermath, and the national decision to let the American South have its way with its former slaves. The boyfriend's comment sparked volumes of remedial reading about American racial history between the end of the Civil War and the next ninety years of Civil Rights struggle—reading that exposed me to information I should have learned (confronted? understood? Comprehended?) in my sophomore course in "American History Since 1865." The bald-faced truth: in 1994, after earning three degrees, after 30 years as a professor, after living through the Civil Rights struggles of the 60s, the reading his "1876" comment inspired revealed that I had spent my adult life knowing almost nothing about how our racial discrimination mess had come to be. To paraphrase Justice Shallow in Shakespeare's *The Merry Wives of Windsor*, "Fie what my ignorance was!" But I've found out that most Americans—otherwise very literate Americans—are at least as ignorant as I was.

It is absolutely crucial that white Americans teach themselves their history, including—I'm tempted to say especially—those parts in which white behavior is most reprehensible. We can't expect African Americans to do it for us, because as Evamarii explained to the Semester at Sea organizer in Chapter 1, doing so sets them up to be resented and dismissed. It's difficult to deny that white people have a long history of killing the messenger. Ignorance of the racial history of our country prevents us from moving forward.

Let's confess: I'm pleased and proud that I undertook, since 1994, to understand racial conditions in Mark Twain's America, that I've struggled to comprehend how lynching and cross burning, how housing and job discrimination, and denial of voting rights, and several other illegal and unconstitutional racial outrages continued for more than ninety years after the Civil War ended, proud that I've tried to thread these elements together and tie them to Twain's relationship to race. And, in turn, I've struggled to connect all of this to my personal process of unlearning racism.

*****

In 1874, when Twain published his account of Auntie Cord's reunion with her son entitled "A True Story," it was eleven years after President Abraham Lincoln had signed the Emancipation Proclamation freeing slaves in the rebellious Confederate states; it was nine years after the end of the Civil War, nine years since Lincoln's assassination, and nine years after the adoption of the Thirteenth Amendment prohibiting slavery; it was seven years after the Fourteenth Amendment confirmed the Civil Rights Act of 1866, which had granted black people the rights and privileges of citizens; and four years after the Fifteenth Amendment forbade denying citizens the right to vote.

All these legal rights were onerous to many Southerners, especially to former slave owners who, by the time of the 1876 election, were required by law to treat them as persons. After the Civil War, U.S. troops and officials occupied the states of the Confederacy in a program called Reconstruction, which amounted to imposing Federal law and order with the objective of enforcing their civil rights, albeit with varying degrees of effectiveness.

In 1876, the South had a legal problem: Congress and the U.S. Constitution required that black people be treated as citizens. The South also had a labor problem: people who once had been compelled by the whip could no longer be forced to work. Freeing the South's slaves had taken away a major portion of the region's property, and now black people had to be paid for their work. And the South had a social problem: people whom many whites considered inferiors because of their race were now entitled to share facilities such as schools and public accommodations from which they previously had been excluded. (To be fair, we must acknowledge that black people were neither uniformly beloved nor respected in the North, either. When the Civil War ended, nineteen of twenty-four Northern states did not allow black people to vote.[34])

The year before "A True Story" was published, an economic depression had begun, a downturn that lasted through the presidential election of 1876, an election that was so closely contested that months afterward ballots were still being counted. In brief, the Democratic candidate, Samuel Tilden, supported by Southern states and a few Northern ones, carried the popular vote by a small margin. Meanwhile, the Republican candidate, Rutherford B. Hayes, had fewer popular votes, but the Electoral College vote remained in dispute. As a result, Tilden's and Hayes's managers negotiated an historic compromise, essentially a quid pro quo, in which Hayes would be awarded the presidency if, in turn, the U.S. government would remove its troops from the South and allow the Southern states to restore the pre-war white supremacy they sought.

There were, however, values upon which many people in the North (except for the so-called Radical Republicans) and in the South agreed. There was a need to build railroads to move the freight that commerce depended on; and that the Union troops that were enforcing Constitutional rights in the South were also needed in the West where there was territory to be claimed from American Indians. It was believed that America could achieve its manifest destiny only if it reallocated money and manpower from Reconstruction in the South to expansion in the West.

In other words, in a time of economic depression so severe that there was unprecedented labor unrest in the North, America decided it couldn't afford to enforce equal rights in the South. In addition to the railroad construction that was needed, there was cotton to be grown and harvested in the South and shipped to Northern mills, and coal to be mined in Alabama and shipped north to fire industrial furnaces. In essence, economic values became more important to the United States than any responsibility to assure by military force that the South's former slaves could vote, work at paying jobs, learn in schools, or serve in government. These were corn-pone issues that trumped civil rights.

Freed by the compromise that settled the presidential election of 1876, Southern Redeemers (whites who sought to restore pre-Civil War white supremacy) imposed their will, essentially without regard to Federal law, for almost eighty years. Southern white power organizations such as the Ku Klux Klan, though small in membership, became culturally powerful. Literacy tests, poll taxes, and intimidation precluded many blacks from exercising their voting rights. Lynching became a common means of punishing black men who were regarded as sexual predators who preyed, or threatened to prey, upon white women. Under slavery it had been common for slave masters to demand sex from slave women; after the Civil War, white Southerners feared that free black men would reciprocate. That fear justified, in many minds, lynching black men who even looked at white women.

Twain in 1876 and After

But how does this 1876 election, this turning point in American history, relate to Mark Twain and his unlearning racism? Let's return to 1874 and Twain's *Atlantic Monthly* narrative, "A True Story," which he published when it still looked likely that Northern Radical Republicans would enforce black civil rights under constitutional guarantees. In 1874, Twain, living in Hartford among Union veterans and former abolitionists, got his corn-pone from writing sympathetically about Auntie Cord; but that was a brief moment: Twain never again wrote for publication with the unmitigated, un-ironic, non-satirical sympathy for black Americans that he expressed so brilliantly and empathically in that essay.

Am I suggesting that Twain joined the many post-Civil War Americans who abandoned southern blacks and their welfare? Did he return to the racism of his youth? No, but, neither did he risk his national popularity by clearly and outspokenly opposing racism. After "A True Story," when his fiction addressed race, he used metaphor, satire, and irony to imply criticism of slavery, segregation, and racism.

The facts are complicated. On the one hand, there's documented evidence Twain supported blacks and their cause, publicly and privately, far more than many Americans of his social class seem to have done during the years after 1876. We know from private correspondence that he believed America's treatment of black people had created a debt of conscience that he and other whites should repay, and we have concrete evidence that he acted on his belief by supporting black individuals and institutions. But paradoxically, he was also a man of his time who occasionally spoke and wrote privately in a way that many of us twenty-first Century Americans would describe as racist. On race, he's complicated. Part of what's fascinating about him is his very inconsistency, his unpredictability, which, if we are to understand his relationship to race, we must explore fearlessly.

Mark Twain's contempt for American Indians lasted a lifetime: he declared it in an 1870 essay, "The Noble Red Man,"[35] which contrasts the romanticized, literary Indian and the "genuine" article he'd experienced out West. He underscored his contempt for Indians in the *Roughing It* passage quoted in Chapter 2, and as late as 1895, in "Fennimore Cooper's Literary Offences" and "Fennimore Cooper's Further Literary Offenses,"[36] he ridiculed Cooper for presenting idealized Indians that Twain believed existed only in fiction.

In private, he was inconsistent regarding black people as well. You'll remember his appreciation for Howells's review of *Roughing It*: "I am as uplifted & reassured by it as a mother who has given birth to a white baby when she was awfully afraid it was going to be a mulatto."[37] In his private notebooks he used the N-word casually, and he occasionally recorded racially offensive jokes. As late as age sixty-one, in 1896, writing from South Africa where he was traveling as part of a round-the-world lecture trip, Twain wrote his friend and benefactor, Henry Huttleston Rogers, on the occasion of Rogers' wedding, joking about the presents he was sending:

> Pair of elephants;
> Pair of rhinoceroses;
> Pair of giraffes;

Pair of zebras;
30 yards of anacondas;
Flock of ostriches;
Herd of niggers.
The wedding-present business is expensive when you work
it from Africa.[38]

Obviously, the letters to Howells and to Rogers were
private, but they betray racial insensitivity nonetheless.

And there is evidence his insensitivity was not merely
momentary. On and off during his last five years, Twain
dictated autobiographical sketches that he intended to be
published after his death, rationalizing that he could speak
freely only from the grave.[39] In a riff on the old-fashioned
minstrel show, he bemoans the absence of a favorite
entertainment, "the real nigger show—the genuine nigger
show, the extravagant nigger show—the show which to me had
no peer and whose peer has not yet arrived, in my
experience."[40] Clearly Twain had the capacity to celebrate, and
apparently enjoyed employing, the word "nigger." On the other
hand, Twain clearly saw himself as a friend of black people, and
acted on his conviction. In December, 1885, he wrote the Dean
of the Yale University School of Law regarding the possibility
of his contributing to the financial support for a promising
black law student, confessing, "I do not believe I would very
cheerfully help a white student who would ask a benevolence of
a stranger, but I do not feel so about the other color. We have
ground the manhood out of them, & the shame is ours, not
theirs, & we should pay for it. If this young man lives as
economically as it is & should be the pride of one to do who is
not straightened, I would like to know what the cost is, so that

I may send 6, 12, or 24 months' board, as the size of the bill may determine."[41]

Professor Shelley Fishkin, in *Lighting Out for the Territory*, explains that the student referred to was Warner T. McGuinn, whom Twain apparently met in 1885 when he spoke at Yale. After studying law at Yale, McGuinn went on to achieve a distinguished career both as a journalist and as an early and effective advocate of black civil rights in Maryland.

Fishkin also tells us that Twain's generosity to black students wasn't limited to McGuinn; there was Charles Ethan Porter, a painter whose studies in Paris Twain supported, and A. W. Jones, a theology student at Lincoln University in Missouri, and there were readings and public appearances at black church fundraising events.[42] Whatever we believe about a man who used the word "nigger" so casually in his personal correspondence, there is ample evidence that he acted on his convictions by furthering black people's interests, individually and collectively.

The paradoxes of Twain's racial behavior penetrated his household as well. The family's Hartford home required numerous servants, notable among them a former slave, George Griffin, who functioned as the household butler for sixteen years. Twain biographers recount several stories about Griffin, but two references to him illustrate Twain's contradictory relationship to race.

The first comes from William Dean Howells, who soon after Twain's death in 1910 memorialized his friend in *My Mark Twain*. Howells describes Twain as a "Southwesterner," raised in a slave community, and he adds, "I never saw a man more regardful of Negroes." In the very next sentence, though, Howells comments tellingly on himself, on Twain, and on the racial attitudes of their times: "He had a yellow butler when I first began to know him, because he said he could not bear to order a white man about, but the terms of his ordering George were those of the softest entreaty which command ever wore."[43] The quote reflects an unselfconscious racial prejudice: on the one hand, Howells found Twain's humane treatment of a black man remarkable and admirable; on the other hand, there's the fact that Twain kept George Griffin as his butler for racist reasons.

Another story of Griffin comes from Shelley Fishkin's *Was Huck Black?* She recounts Twain visiting New York City in 1893, a time of national economic depression, two years after the family had closed their Hartford home and begun a series of European residencies in search of health cures and cheaper living costs. Twain, in the city for business purposes, met Griffin at Twain's New York hotel, whereupon they walked about the city. Griffin was "faultlessly dressed," and Twain remarked that he seemed to be doing well financially, making loans to people "of his own race" and to white men who were financially desperate. Griffin, however, was "a prosperous & happy person & about the only one thus conditioned I met in New York."[44] Fishkin quotes Twain's account of taking Griffin to the offices of *Century Magazine* and *St. Nicholas Magazine* where they were received with curiosity, the public companionship of a black man and a white gentleman of Twain's celebrity being a rarity even in New York City. Twain adds:

The glances embarrassed George, but not me, for the companionship was proper; in some ways he was my equal, in some others my superior; & besides, deep down in my interior I knew that the difference between any two of those poor transient things called human beings that have ever crawled about this world & then hid their little vanities in the compassionate shelter of the grave was but microscopic, trivial, a mere difference between worms.[45]

Fishkin speculates, not unreasonably, that Twain was recognizing the absurdity of racial categories, and she's probably right, which puts Twain far ahead of his peers, but the incident can also be seen from another perspective. An argument can be made that Twain was also being carelessly insensitive toward Griffin, who may have found this public flaunting of the social contract personally dangerous. What Twain described as George's embarrassment may have been concern on Griffin's part that he might have to pay a future price for having crossed Jim Crow social boundaries.

This is not to challenge Twain's admiration for black people and their achievements. Clearly he respected Griffin's financial acumen, just as he respected Jerry and his "Corn-pone Opinions." In fact, it's possible Twain believed literally that Jerry, the woodpile preacher, was the "greatest orator in the United States." In addition to his respect for Griffin and Jerry, Twain maintained a self-professed, life-long admiration for John Lewis, a black Quarry Farm employee who single-handedly stopped a runaway carriage carrying family members and a servant. Ron Powers, in his carefully researched and brilliantly written biography of Twain, reports:

No one was more transported by the rescue than Sam Clemens. Lewis had performed an act appropriate to the pages of an adventure book that Sammy Clemens had read—or that Mark Twain might write. In fact, Mark Twain did write it, in versions that appeared in *Pudd'nhead Wilson* and *Life on the Mississippi*. He formed a friendship with Lewis that lasted until the farmer's death in 1906.

But Powers also points out Twain's capacity to categorize about Lewis and about black people:

> He reported that when someone asked him whether a watch would be "a wise gift" for the black man, "I said, 'Yes, the very wisest of all; I know the colored race, & know that in Lewis's eyes this fine toy will throw the other more valuable testimonies far away into the shade.' But he added, "[&] if any scoffer shall say 'Behold this thing is out of character,' there is an inscription within, which will silence him; for it will teach him that this wearer aggrandizes the watch, not the watch the wearer."[46]

His comment about knowing the "colored race," and Lewis's valuing the "toy" is insulting to Lewis and it stereotypes black people, but just as he was capable of racially-insensitive language, he was also loyal and generous for a lifetime to those, like Lewis, whom he believed to be faithful to him.

But what about Twain's treatment of race in his writing after 1876? Today *The Adventures of Huckleberry Finn* is considered Twain's greatest novel. Narrated by an uneducated Missouri boy (Huckleberry) who is befriended by an escaped slave (Jim), the novel traces their adventures and emerging friendship. When it was banned from libraries in Concord, Massachusetts, and Brooklyn, New York, not long after its 1885 publication, *Huckleberry Finn* was attacked not for its treatment of race, but because of Huckleberry's bad grammar and his unsuitability as a role model for youth. Only after World War II did *Huckleberry Finn* come under serious attack for its insensitive treatment of black people, specifically for the scores of times the N-word appears—some cite more than two hundred. Many who find the book racially offensive, cite not only the use of that offensive term but also Twain's portrayal of the slave Jim as superstitious and illiterate.

Writers who take sides about the book's treatment of race disagree over whether these issues constitute racism on Twain's part. Defenders justify the word as being realistic for its time, and they assert that Jim is the novel's most heroic and admirable character. They defend the book, claiming that Jim's behavior is strategic and tactical—an adaptive behavior learned by slaves who were powerless in a white-dominated South.

Many, including I, believe that *The Adventures of Huckleberry Finn* contains a thinly concealed, ironic attack on antebellum treatment of former slaves. But Twain's sympathy for the slave Jim, who serves as Huck's companion and sometime lifesaver, is indirect and ironic. It is not the openly expressed sympathy of "A True Story." For example, Huckleberry marvels at Jim's love for family, surprised that a slave is capable of such humanity. Huck doesn't question the legitimacy of slavery, and never in the novel does he advocate for the humane treatment of slaves. Twain, a professional writer who earned his living from book sales and lecture fees, doesn't allow Huck to offer direct praise for Jim as a truly heroic and generous man. Instead, Twain assumes, or gambles, that readers will understand that he's dealing in indirection, depending on metaphor and irony. Given that he began *The Adventures of Huckleberry Finn* in 1876 at a time when many of his Northern and Southern readers might reject a novel that directly challenged post-1876 racial attitudes, this approach perhaps makes financial, if not moral, sense.

Those who object to Twain's stereotyping Jim as an ignorant and superstitious buffoon would be even more offended if they were to study *Tom Sawyer Abroad*, Twain's 1892 attempt to revive the adventures of Tom, Huck, and Jim, in which the black man, Jim, is given almost none of the dignity that offsets the racial stereotyping found in *The Adventures of Huckleberry Finn*. Nat Hentoff, in his introduction to The Oxford Mark Twain edition of *Tom Sawyer Abroad* says, "except in a few pages, [Jim] could have been played by Stepin Fetchit."[47] Hentoff is not exaggerating. There is every reason to believe Twain was using Tom, Huck, and Jim to get money he needed desperately if he was to protect himself and his family from bankruptcy. It seems to be a corn-pone potboiler that is almost impossible to defend against charges of using racial stereotyping in order to get cheap laughs.

Twain's other major novel that explores slavery and racial prejudice in the antebellum South is *The Tragedy of Pudd'nhead Wilson and the Comedy of Those Extraordinary Twins*. The book consists of two stories, published in one volume in 1894; of the two, the text that deals directly with race is *Pudd'nhead Wilson*.[48]

If post-Reconstruction conditions were horrible for black people when *Huckleberry Finn* was published in 1885, they were worse by 1894 when *The Tragedy of Pudd'nhead Wilson* appeared; it is estimated that in 1892, the year Twain began working on *Pudd'nhead*, there were one hundred sixty-one lynchings of black Americans.[49] In it, he depended on indirect-tion, metaphor, and irony at least as much as he had in *Huckleberry Finn*. *Pudd'nhead* is a fascinating mess of a novel that intertwines a spaghetti bowl of subjects including miscegenation, slavery, prejudice, antebellum Southern aristocratic values, heredity versus training, and complexities of parental love. Given the virulent Jim Crow racism of the 1890s in America, there was little chance Twain could have made money from publishing a novel that was a frontal attack on racial prejudice. So, as with *Huckleberry Finn*, he set it in the past — the South of the 1850s — affording him opportunity to raise complicated questions about nature, nurture, and the other themes described above. The pre-Civil War setting al-lowed him to avoid direct criticism of post-war white racism, while coming close by ironically exploring the racist notion that a drop of black blood pumping in an individual legitimized discrimination against that person.

Concerning Twain and the Jews

When he wrote in *The Innocents Abroad* about his 1867 visit to the Holy Land, Twain iconoclastically contrasted the Holy Land that travel literature had prepared him with the places he actually experienced: Jerusalem was tiny; beggars were everywhere; Jews and Muslims were poor, shabby, and often diseased; and the Christian Pilgrims with whom he was traveling were vandals. His ability to write humorously about these experiences surprised some, shocked others, and entertained many, fueling his rapid rise to international recognition.

Thirty years later Twain had a different kind of encounter with Jews, this time in Europe. Beginning in the fall of 1897 he and his family spent about twenty months in Vienna, Austria, in the midst of pervasive, vicious anti-Semitism that we now realize led inexorably to Adolph Hitler, Nazism, and death camps. In 1896, Sam and Livy's favorite daughter Susy had died of spinal meningitis; middle-daughter Clara wanted desperately to study piano in Vienna; Henry Huttleston Rogers had found ways to lift the family out of bankruptcy, leaving Twain and Livy essentially debt free. Supposedly Twain's international celebrity made it impossible for him to write while living in London, so they removed to Vienna. The family's stay in Vienna failed to deliver him from the demands of celebrity, but Clara successfully pursued her piano training, through which she met a fellow student, Ossip Grabrilowitsch, whom she eventually married.

Ron Powers describes the Austrian capital of 1897 as "a vortex of historic transformation...at once a world center of art, thought, and café-society elegance" as well as a central battlefield on which the 'Jewish Question' smoldered toward conflagration."[50] East European Jews had fled to the West in the 1880s, avoiding pogroms in Poland and Russia; the West was in the midst of an economic depression (nearly always a problematic time for immigrants); and the Dreyfus trials in Paris were capturing international attention.

When he first settled into Viennese life, Twain was welcomed, but within weeks he began to be lampooned, both pictorially and verbally, as "Mark Twain the Jew" by the powerful anti-Semite portion of the press. Twain provided *Harpers Monthly* with an article entitled "Stirring Times in Austria," which dealt with Vienna's politics. In it, he described a parliamentarian who threatened to box another's ears, to which the member announced he'd "rather take my hat off to a Jew" than bow to his opponent; another added, "Jew flunky! Here we have been fighting the Jews for ten years, and now you are helping them to power again. How much do you get for it?"[51]

In the same *Harpers* article, Twain committed one of his "Ready! Fire! Aim!" offenses by generalizing carelessly about Jews, their persecution, and their history when he declared that American Jews had not served as vitally as they should have in American military efforts. Subsequently, in another article entitled "Concerning the Jews," he acknowledged that he'd erred in "High Times in Austria," but then he dug himself into an even deeper hole by declaring himself free of prejudice — except toward the French:

> I am quite sure I have no race prejudices, and I think I have no color prejudices, nor caste prejudices nor creed prejudices. Indeed, I know it. I can stand any society. All that I care to know is that a man is a human being—that is enough for me; he can't be any worse. I have no special regard for Satan; but I can at least lay claim that I have no prejudice against him. It may be that I lean a little his way, on account of his not having a fair show. All religions issue bibles against him, and say the most injurious things about

him, but we never hear his side. We have none but the evidence for the prosecution, and yet we have rendered the verdict. To my mind, this is irregular. It is un-English; it is un-American; it is French. Without this precedent Dreyfus could not have been condemned.[52]

To that point in the essay, he'd done himself little or no harm in relation to Jewish readers and sympathizers, but alas, he followed it with a series of generalizations about Jews, all delivered with Twainian certainty, but essentially unsupported by anything other than his personal perception. The most offensive assertion, and the one that has been condemned most frequently to this day, was his conviction that Jews have been hated and persecuted throughout history because they excel at making money. Since "the morning of time," Twain declared, Jews have understood that all men worship money, and "the cost to him has been heavy; his success has made the whole human race his enemy."[53]

Did he mean well toward Jews? I believe so. Was this typical of him? Yes, in the same way that he could casually refer to "niggers" in his private correspondence, and at the same time believe himself to be without prejudice of color or race. He was a brilliant man, a genius of a unique sort, but a man sometimes shockingly lacking in self-awareness.

In this 1899 effort to support Jews and to explain Vienna's anti-Semitism to his American readers, however, Twain exhibited a new and different relationship to his corn-pone. After all, his was an effort to defend Jews against hatred. Yes, he may have done it in a way that led some Jews to feel they'd rather not be befriended. Nevertheless, one can argue that

"Concerning the Jews" represented his first openly, non-ironic, non-satirical public defense of an ethnic minority since "A True Story."

Chapter Six

Enter Evamarii

"You can never relax; you can never let your guard down. It's a wonder every black person in this country isn't insane."
— Evamarii Johnson

When Evamarii and I married in 1984, I entered what were for me uncharted waters: I'd never dated a black woman. She had dated white men before, so she had a clearer notion of what we might encounter. I was uncertain how my children, my parents, my friends, and my colleagues would respond. As it turned out, only my mother was a problem. My son and daughter, Christopher and Juliet, were fine with it, as were my friends and colleagues. Race was never a problem for the people I cared most about.

I am without a doubt a richer person because of our marriage. I've met people whom I wouldn't have met otherwise. I've been in social situations that most white people have never experienced. I've also had some disappointing experiences, mostly with white folks.

First, though, I'll describe a brief and fairly casual exchange between Evamarii and me that I believe was a central inspiration for writing this book. In either 1986 or 1987, Evamarii and I were watching the PBS evening news as they showed the final moments of a confrontation between Klan marchers and black counter-demonstrators that had climaxed in fisticuffs and police intervention. The mini-drama's denouement involved a white man in his twenties proclaiming to the camera something to the effect that, "My people got a right to be here, got a right to march, and they ain't got a right to tell us we can't." I think we were to assume his "people" were the Klansmen and their vocal white supporters, and the "they" who had no right to disagree were people, black and white, who objected to the Klan and its bigotry.

Without forethought I commented, "I've wondered whether my Grandpa Pritner was a Klansman. When I was a teenager I asked him and Grandma about the Klan, and I remember them saying that the Klan had done some good things. It's something I've wondered about. "

"Were they racist?"

"Oh, yeah! At least he was. " It may have been the first time in forty years that I'd thought of Grandpa telling the Rastus joke. "He had a sense of humor. He was a joker, and some of his jokes were pretty raw on race." My face must have betrayed some additional thoughts, because Evamarii looked at me for a few seconds, and then said, "I hope I don't find out some day that you did racist things. That would be so disappointing."

"I don't think so," I replied. I recall vividly that in the moment I remembered no specifics that I could or should confess to, but neither was I as confident as I wished.

A dozen years later, after I'd begun performing "Mark Twain: Traveling," a humorous one-person performance as Twain, I began creating the serious piece, "Mark Twain: Unlearning Racism." One evening I was fitting together passages from his writing when the phrase "throw eggs at niggers" bubbled up out of some long-concealed wrinkle of memory. I'm grateful that it did, grateful that the phrase inspired me to confront the ugliest of my racial memories, grateful that some part of my lizard brain had stored that incident and the phrase associated with it for forty-some years. I remember so vividly that I associated the phrase first with the television experience and Evamarii's saying she hoped I'd never done "racist things." I'd hidden that memory from myself, tricked myself into believing in a false version of who I'd been. Of course, I'm not thankful that I participated in an ugly racist incident; I wish profoundly that I hadn't. But retrieving and confronting that memory set the synapses to connecting—that memory inspired my self-examination—provoking a question that I've spent more than a decade addressing: "How did I go about unlearning my racism?"

Surprisingly though—at least surprisingly to me—race has never been a significant factor, day to day, within in our marriage. In fact, our biggest differences have nothing to do with race and little to do with gender. I'm a slow-paced Midwesterner from Kansas, and she's a fast-thinking, fast-talking Easterner from New Jersey. Sometimes that can be a challenge!

We've experienced few abrasive incidents related to our being an interracial couple. A couple of comments have come from black men — strangers who felt obliged to announce their feelings about a white man being with a black woman. On the other hand, in Bloomington and Normal, where we were living, there were half a dozen occasions when Evamarii noticed stares from older white folks in restaurants. On those occasions she responded to the lingering attention by asking, loudly enough to be heard, "Calvin, do we know those people?" I learned to laugh at the white folks' surprise at her willingness to confront their rude stares.

Once, in a pub in London I missed out on a tirade from a drunken Londoner, a white woman who sat by her male partner in a Notting Hill Gate pub pursuing a tipsy monologue, sotto voce, that I learned the details of only after exiting. Strolling toward our tube station, Evamarii asked, "Why didn't you say anything in there?"

"About what?"

"That woman."

"What are you talking about?" I was totally baffled.

"That woman sat there and called me everything but a child of God for half an hour; and you didn't say a word."

"Evamarii, I barely understand a fraction of what these folks say. I had no idea it was going on. I'm terribly sorry, but I can't be held responsible for what I don't know about. I don't know what I would have done, but I didn't understand any of it. I just heard her jabbering and I paid no attention." And while that was completely true, now I see that it may also be true that ignoring what other people are saying might be something I can do because I'm white and male and have the privilege of not caring what other people think.

In the spring of 1986, Evamarii and I drove to Richmond, Virginia, to see my daughter, Juliet, play Miranda in a production of Shakespeare's *The Tempest*. Returning to Illinois through the mountains of West Virginia, we chose a winding two-lane route intended to save us several miles of driving while also providing a scenic alternative to the interstate we'd taken going east. I drove slowly, enjoying the mountain and river views. Then, perhaps ten miles into the scenic drive, we each noticed that we were being followed by a helmeted two-hundred-and-seventy pounder on a huge, thundering motor-cycle—the kind with the high handlebars. It's perhaps the only time I've thought, "I wish I had a billy club or a baseball bat in this car." Ultimately, the experience was only mildly intimidating. Three or four times, Motorcycle Boy pulled to within a threatening car-length behind us, roaring his pipes to demand our attention; at other times he fell back as much as fifty yards.

All the while, I drove the tightly curving road, paying almost no attention to the scenery we'd sought, steering while glancing briefly in the rearview mirrors, approximating the speed limit, wondering what intention our trailing motorcyclist had rattling around in his pea brain. Frightened? Not really, but neither of us commented on the situation until Motorcycle Boy turned away a mile or two before we encountered the interstate. Later we agreed that we'd had pretty much the same experience: believing we weren't in danger, but knowing we were in the presence of a mindless man who probably had the capacity to do great harm. Neither of us was going to be provoked into doing something stupid.

Another memorable incident came five years later, when Evamarii and I were driving from our home in Evanston, Illinois, to Louisville, Kentucky, for the Humana Theatre Festival. We were bypassing Indianapolis on a cloudy Friday morning in moderate traffic on the interstate west of the city. I stayed in sync with the three-lane flow, easing off as the traffic clogged occasionally, slowing us all to the posted speed limit, fifty-five, but mostly we all sped up to the mid-sixties, maintaining an informal herd that inched past one another at one moment, fell behind at another, but mostly held together at a steady pace. Traveling about sixty, I came upon a slower car in the center lane, pulled left to pass, then edged back to the center lane, rejoining the rhythm that ebbed and flowed. A moment later I checked my mirrors and registered immediately that a light on top of an unmarked sedan behind me was flashing, which I took to be a signal for me to pull over, which I did. Recognizing the sedan as one that had been in the traffic flow for the last several miles, I climbed out and stood by our Toyota, while from the sedan there emerged a thirty-something fellow dressed in camouflage fatigues, black combat-style boots, with a camouflage duckbill cap perched atop a roundish face that was supported by a fleshy neck. At first I read the costume as that of a National Guardsman who was headed to or from his weekend warrior duties. But then I saw that there were no military insignias on the uniform, no name on the shirt, and no insignia on the cap. Militia? Pink-faced and slightly pot-bellied, he maintained his version of martial presence as he swaggered toward me, traffic ticket folder in hand. I asked, "Is there something wrong?" No response. He paused to bend over and stare in at Evamarii for several seconds, raised to an erect posture with his folder in hand before him, and looked evenly at me. "You were doing seventy in a fifty-five mile an hour zone." There was a long silence on both our parts.

I knew he'd win. There was no independent witness I could tap to prove that Camouflage Man and I had been driving at approximately the same speed for at least five miles until I passed that one car. It was his word against mine, and I wasn't going to come out ahead. I said nothing. He looked at me intently, showing the faintest smirk, before he looked down and began writing out the ticket. I maintained silence.

When he completed the write-up he carefully tore off the top copy and handed it to me. I accepted it, glanced at the numbers, 55 and 70, then stood silently, gazing without confronting, intending to communicate that I knew this was about a white man with a black woman in a car, and that it was race that bothered him. But I wasn't going to utter a challenging word. He understood, and when he saw I wasn't going to risk belligerence, he turned and walked back to his vehicle, opened the door, turned and stood staring at me for a couple of beats.

Now it was my turn to move, so I climbed in, fired up the Celica, engaged the left turn signal, and eased onto the highway, driving a steady fifty-five as car after car passed us doing the sixty and sixty-five or so that had been the norm fifteen minutes earlier. Only he kept up the fifty-five mile an hour pace behind me until I engaged the right turn signal announcing that I was headed south on the interstate toward Louisville. There we parted.

In 1995, I left retirement to chair the theatre department at the University of Missouri/Kansas City. The decision was a quick one that we made literally during the previous summer as we were on our way to our regular summer teaching job with gifted high school students, to be followed by a guest-teaching semester in the fall at the California Institute of the Arts. In January, I moved a minimum of furniture into our Kansas City apartment where I lived alone for a few weeks while Evamarii took responsibility for selling our Evanston condominium and moving our possessions. Our apartment was in one of the classier residential complexes in Kansas City, a full-service, doorman building, five-minute walk from the J. C. Nichols Plaza, and ten-minute walk from my office—a delightful situation for a couple of folks who see themselves as city rats.

For a few weeks, I stayed in a one-bedroom furnished apartment the management supplied temporarily while the management painted and re-carpeted the two bedroom, two bath, balconied place we were to occupy. The condo sold quickly; Evamarii packed and shipped our belongings (mostly books), and drove to Kansas City, arriving the day before the movers. On the second day of her and my occupation of the newly refurbished apartment, I came home from work in the late afternoon, and Evamarii greeted me in scruffy clothes appropriate to the process of unpacking: "I have to tell you what happened!" she announced. "The lady—Mary—the one who works with Guest Services, knocked. I answered, and stood in the doorway. She looked at me, surprised, said, 'Is Mister Pritner home?' I knew immediately she thought 'black woman, cleaning woman,' or maybe I was there for the laundry. Who knows? But I kept a straight face, absolutely innocent. I wasn't about to tell her who I was. I said, 'No, Mr. Pritner isn't here.' She had a plant in her hands—that one," she pointed. "Clearly, she didn't know what to say; maybe I was your mistress, but I was dressed in an old sweatshirt and slacks, so that didn't look likely. So, finally she offered the plant, and said, 'Please tell Mister Pritner I brought this, and I wanted to welcome him.' I said I'd tell you. Some day she'll figure out we're married," Evamarii concluded, "and then she'll be fawning all over me!"

And she was right. Within days we passed Mary in the lobby and she tried to engage Evamarii in conversation, but the friendliness was reciprocated with formality. The woman deserved to sweat for her misguided assumptions, whatever they were, and Evamarii proved more than willing to feed the discomfort.

The personal experiences of race that seem to bother her most are those like the interaction with Guest Services Mary in which she is treated not as an individual, but as a "black woman." After a lifetime of it, she still finds the racial stereotyping shocking. "It can come out of nowhere," she explains. "Here I am, just being me, being myself, and it happens again. You can never relax; you can never let your guard down. It's a wonder every black person in this country isn't insane." It may come when she's shopping in a department store, dressed comparably to the other middle-class folks in the store, and she realizes that she's being followed—one would guess by a person who's on the lookout for shoplifters. The little old white ladies in our fancy Kansas City apartment building often shifted their purses from one side to another, protecting them, when she entered the elevator. After one of those elevator incidents she'd say, "I want to ask her 'can't you imagine I live in this building too? Is it that hard for you to imagine that a middle-aged black woman can live in this building, ride the elevator with you, and can you imagine that it doesn't occur to me that you have anything to worry about until you hide that purse?'"

What's the answer? Will people of different races ever be able to live comfortably with each other, able to see each other as individuals? Obviously, some already do. But for some, it will take time and patience, and for others it will require self-conscious effort.

Evamarii and I live in a predominantly Dominican neighborhood in upper Manhattan – Washington Heights, just above Harlem. On most days I see more brown and black people than I do white people. At my gym, a dozen blocks away on 181st Street, El Grande Gimnasio, I'm usually the only old white guy there. Nobody bothers me. I don't bother anybody. It's not a big deal.

Across the street from our apartment is Coogan's, a restaurant and bar owned and operated by three friendly Irish-Americans who employ a mix of Dominicans, African Americans and white folks from the U.S. and from abroad. The clientele comes from our densely populated neighborhood, as well as from New York Presbyterian Hospital staff and from the medical school and nursing school students; it's not unusual to see residents in their green hospital garb. The first time we went there, Evamarii overheard gossip on the part of two Democratic Party politicos. Everyone is there. On the wall there's a Manny Ramirez baseball jersey from his Cleveland Indians years—Manny's from the neighborhood. In 2001, Coogan's was honored, among 5000 entries, as the best neighborhood restaurant in the United States. Why? It's the food and the prices and the clientele. It's the weekly Latino-Irish Karaoke Night. I think most importantly it's the Salsa, Blues, and Shamrocks 5K run that David Hunt, Peter Walsh, and Tess O'Conner Dade, Coogan's owners, sponsored each March. This is a neighborhood place in which several ethnicities and religions and nationalities find a way to be together comfortably. If every American neighborhood had a mix like ours, and a Coogan's, maybe America would be different. 54

Over the last few years as I've explored Twain and race, and my relationship to race, reading widely but not always in a well-organized fashion, I've come to realize that there's probably no question that I've wondered about that hasn't been researched, and often quantified, by sociologists, educators, or historians. The facts are there and they're worth seeking out – for those who want to teach themselves.

I've been going weekly to a support group related to an ongoing medical problem that I've had for years. One day in the group, we got somehow onto the subject of race. A long-term member, a fellow my age, said, "I've always wondered why the blacks didn't just go back to Africa after the Civil War, after they were free." Heads sort of ducked. Nobody responded. The topic changed. I can't be sure why nobody said anything, but I'm reasonably confident that some folks just don't want to touch that third rail of race. It's too easy to get burned.

Why didn't I answer? I think it was because it would have taken too long to answer him, and because I didn't believe he wanted an answer, or at least not the answer I would have given. I would have had to go carefully, step by step, through the massive problems that existed for black Freedmen in 1865 and the years immediately thereafter.

The Freedmen had no money—not very little money—they had none; almost certainly many had never handled money; they didn't have the money to get to the North and look for work, let alone have the money to hire a ship and cross the Atlantic to a continent with which the U.S. had little economic exchange. Few Freedmen had skills that they could exchange for money in a South that lost most of its resources in the war; after all, before the Civil War, slaves themselves had been the most financially valuable "property" in the South. Culturally, few Freedmen had specific knowledge of where in Africa their ancestors had been captured, kidnapped, shipped, and sold; in a sense, they knew themselves simply as people who had been bought and sold, worked and punished by a slave master from dawn to dusk all their lives.

It would have taken the group's entire session to talk the fellow's question through; and I wasn't sure it was really a question so much as it was possibly the expression of a desire that race and the problem of race would go away.

If I wish I'd said anything, I wish I'd simply said, "If you'd like, I've been doing a lot of reading about race and those times. I'd certainly be willing to talk with you about what the slaves faced after the Civil War. " Yes, I wish I'd said that, and that I'd told him about some things he could read. Instead, I keep going over this in my mind.

To Teach: An Intransitive Verb

Except for a couple of years in the Navy, I've been on the teaching side of education since 1957. The best learning about race that I've observed took place in a most unlikely setting: among students in a professional actor training program.

From 1995 to 2000, Evamarii and I lived in Kansas City while I taught and administered for a professionally-oriented graduate theatre program. A few days after I got there in January my colleague, Louis Colaianni, gathered the graduate acting program's students and most of their teachers in the early afternoon of Martin Luther King Day, the national holiday that the University recognized by dismissing classes. Each year Louis asked the first year Master of Fine Arts acting students to present an hour's reflections on Dr. King's significance, so that rather than merely taking a holiday from classes, we gathered to fulfill what Louis considered to be the purpose of the holiday: reflection on King's life and contributions.

Each year's presentation was unique, because the students found very personal ways of celebrating King. That first year there was a modern dance created by a talented black woman; others read aloud from King's sermons and letters; I remember there being video of Chicago ethnic whites attacking Dr. King and his associates at a demonstration related to housing discrimination. Another year I remember a video collage that included the same white rioters in Chicago, police and dogs in the South (probably Bull Connor and his police in Birmingham) attacking black and white demonstrators; almost always there was the March on Washington.

The students (white, black, and Latinx students, all of them college graduates in their mid-twenties) regularly described having known of Dr. King, having studied about King and the civil rights movement in school, but having only the haziest awareness of the specifics of King's struggles against discrimination. Each year one or more of these graduate students reported that this acting school event was their first in-depth exploration of the rabid violence Dr. King was subjected to in the North. They'd known of white attacks on King and his associates in the South, but they'd known little of the strong Northern resistance. By asking the students to create a program about Dr. King, Louis devised a situation in which these young women and men taught themselves.

Let's face it, many of these acting students had attended high schools as well as colleges and universities whose teachers had avoided involving themselves more than necessary with an issue that might threaten their corn-pone. So, we continue to have citizens who have only the fuzziest awareness of 20th-Century America's history of racism North and South, East and

West: lynchings, cross burnings, red-lining real estate agents, job discrimination, and segregated schools that were commonplace for decades.

I came to admire Louis's strategy for dealing with the national holiday and the day off from classes: the students taught themselves about Dr. King and the civil rights struggle, and we, their teachers, were reminded of our own need to keep learning, to keep informing ourselves. It was the best kind of teaching—directed self-education shared with sympathetic peers. Louis's strategy was probably the best I've experienced: he was a white man asking the students to teach themselves and share their learning.

One way I taught myself as part of writing this book was by watching movies, specifically, *Birth of a Nation*, *Gone with the Wind*, *Song of the South*, and *The Defiant Ones*. I love movies. I love the emotional connection movies can draw me into. So, I thought, "Let's see how these movies reflect America's relationship to race and to my unlearning racism?"

Birth of a Nation, a silent film that was originally released in 1915, was based on Thomas Dixon's novels *The Clansman* and *The Leopard's Spots*. Historians consider it one of the great dramatic films of all time—massive in its innovation, and powerful in both its technical and aesthetic influences on future filmmakers. While influential it may be, when I viewed the entirety of *Birth of a Nation* for the first time in 2005, ninety years after its release, I was left with a thimble full of positive aesthetic reaction, compared to a cup overloaded with social and political disgust.

It's Griffith's twisted, prejudiced version of American racial history, a biased representation of Reconstruction and its aftermath, a blatant stereotyping of Civil War and Reconstruction, black people presented as mindless cotton pickers on the old plantation, played by wooly-wigged white actors in blackface, who subsequently become rapacious black bucks who almost literally salivate over the idea of raping defenseless white women. Griffith's film gives us crooked, slovenly black, Reconstruction-elected officials, and it glorifies the "gallant" men of the Ku Klux Klan as saviors of white women. I found the film repulsive and its presentation of blacks is uniformly negative, but I also felt that way because I knew that the film had profoundly influenced American attitudes toward black people for generations.

Birth of a Nation grossed the greatest box office receipts of any film up to that time; President Woodrow Wilson, a Southerner by birth and culture, praised its historical accuracy. The three-hour story's romantic ending joins a pure Northern girl, Elsie, with a brave Southerner, Ben, in a poetic tableau that symbolically brings formerly warring factions together in peace and love. It's a film that idealizes a fairly blatant consensus, a North/South consensus that treats black freedom as a dangerous impulse that must be suppressed, and a consensus that celebrates white virtue. It may be technically brilliant, but for me it's an aesthetic success put to evil purposes.

The first movie I remember seeing as a child was *Gone with the Wind*. It scared me so much that my vivid memory is one of peeking through the space between two seats, crouching to see, then turning away from the screen, and then peering back at wartime scenes of bombs exploding, wagons crashing, and horses whinnying. I can't swear my father was there beside me, but I've no memory of Mother ever going to a movie with Dad and me—so, it's a good bet he had taken me. I didn't see it again until the spring or summer of 1954 when Jackie and I saw it in re-release at a Kansas City drive-in. I have no memory of being offended by its treatment of race and slavery—a testament, I suppose, to my college boy insensitivity. But when I viewed it on a laser disk at the California Institute of the Arts in July 2006, I saw it almost as a totally different movie.

From the opening credits, I realized that *Gone with the Wind* is a story told from a Southern point of view. My notes, scribbled in the dark, read: "Opens with a description of the setting, a 'land of Cavaliers and cotton fields called the Old South' where 'Gallantry took its last bow' the 'last ever to be seen of Knights and their Ladies Fair, of Master and Slave,' 'Look for it only in books, for it is no more than a dream remembered' and 'a civilization gone with the wind.'" The verbal clichés function as a trumpet call announcing a parade of stereotypes: loyal slaves, kindly but stern masters and mistresses, rapacious carpetbaggers, greedy white Northerners—and let us not forget Prissy, played by Butterfly McQueen, who pleads in panic, "I don't know nuth'n 'bout birthin' babies."

Re-released six times, it's one of the most popular films ever—and, let's face it, part of the reason for its popularity may well be the comfortable consensus view of racial history that it presents—a consensus that I'd describe as saying, "Yes, slavery wasn't quite right, but there were faults in the North as well as in the South. And, isn't it wonderful how the South's white folks looked after their black folks?" I'm convinced that for many white Americans of my generation, the film continues to influence their attitudes toward black people—for some, helping them yearn for a day when black folks knew their place.

The same week I saw *Gone with the Wind*, I watched a movie that I'd seen as an eleven-year-old: Disney's 1946 *Song of the South*, the company's first film to intersperse animation with live action. Like *Birth of a Nation* and *Gone With the Wind*, it's a technical marvel, but from my 21st Century liberal point of view it's a social disaster. My notes suggest that I literally couldn't tell whether it was supposed to be taking place before or after the Civil War; the black characters are happy-go-lucky stereotypes who are absolutely dedicated to the welfare of their loving white masters and the white children who adore them. The movie's mixture of animation and live action is technically brilliant, albeit the innovation does nothing to further the storytelling. And, not unimportantly for a comfortable consensus view of the South, the story is life affirming: the Uncle Remus character, adapted from Joel Chandler Harris's 19th-Century Southern fiction, is the most generous and humane character in the story. Of course, he's a stereotypical loyal former slave.

In short, *Song of the South* is a 1946 affirmation of a racially prejudiced point of view about black people. After spending a substantial amount of time searching the internet for information about the movie's racial background, the most telling quote I found was at the Georgia Humanities Council's website,

> There was much discussion within the Disney studio about how the story and the African American characters should

be presented. One of the scriptwriters, Clarence Muse—an African American—urged that black characters in the film be portrayed in a positive light. He was so disappointed in the response he received that he resigned before the script was complete. That the studio was not concerned with making a racially progressive statement was perhaps reflected in its choice of James Baskett, an actor in the *Amos and Andy* radio show, to play Uncle Remus, and in Walt Disney's comment to a colleague that he had hired a "swell little pickaninny" to play a black child in the film. [55]

My week at the movies ended with *The Defiant Ones*, a film that I believe contributed substantially to my unlearning racism. As sophomoric as it may sound to admit it, when I saw *The Defiant Ones*, in Washington, DC, in 1959, it was both emotionally moving and socially revelatory.

A dramatic film that's told from a blatantly pro-integration point of view, the story involves two convicts, white Johnny "Joker" Jackson (Tony Curtis) and black Noah Cullen (Sidney Poitier) who escape a Southern chain gang handcuffed together, and who, in order to survive, learn to overcome their prejudices toward each other. It is both a tragic and an uplifting story that ends memorably: Poitier manages to climb aboard a moving train and reaches back to help the white man climb aboard; but when Poitier fails in his struggle to bring Curtis aboard, he jumps off to help him, knowing that by doing so they'll both be captured and, at best, returned to prison. The image of Poitier reaching back for Curtis, of the black and white hands clutching each other, is one of the most powerful in my film memory. As maudlin and romantic as it may be to admit it, the film profoundly and permanently affected my attitude toward race relations.

On the other hand, viewing the movie almost fifty years later, remembering how it inspired me to think in a newly humanistic way about race and race relations, I was pleased that it's a good piece of filmmaking. Its cinematographer and screenwriter won Oscars; Curtis, Poitier, Theodore Bikel, and Cara Williams were nominated for acting; Stanley Kramer was nominated for best director; and both the editor and the film were nominated as well – not bad for a movie that celebrated a humanistic black and white relationship, with an integrationist point of view, in 1959, well before we think of the movie industry moving to the liberal side of racial matters. The film's ending, however, with the black character selflessly sacrificing himself and his freedom for his white companion, may have had a hand in making the integrationist message easier for a popular audience to accept. And making it the story of escaped convicts kept the story resolutely beyond everyday life in a way that another Poitier movie made eight years later, *Guess Who's Coming to Dinner*, did not. Like Twain, Hollywood could not risk it's corn-pone too directly.

Conclusion

I've achieved with this book what I set out to do: describe how Mark Twain and I worked toward unlearning our racism. The book's successes and failures must be left for others to address. I feel, however, a responsibility to offer suggestions for others in their struggles to identify and cast off the bits of racism they find in themselves. I shall resist the impulse to direct others toward a path they may follow. To paraphrase

Twain, who spoke on the occasion of his seventieth birthday at Delmonico's restaurant in New York City, I've gotten where I am by following a path that would be wrong for another person—nobody can get there by following the road I've taken. Twain followed his path—and I've followed mine, each of us succeeding and failing, following his corn-pone path. Besides, I still believe that to teach is an intransitive verb. In that mode, I'll end by describing one of my most successful teaching experiences.

I took a year off from graduate school in 1961-1962 and returned to Kansas City where I taught high school English and journalism. After a semester of helping the students get their weekly newspaper up and running, I found myself wanting to challenge them to move beyond received ideas and to become independent thinkers. In the spring, President John F. Kennedy and Roger Blough, President of the U.S. Steel Corporation became involved in a confrontation over Kennedy's conviction that Blough had double-crossed both Kennedy and the steel workers' union. Kennedy had convinced the union to take a smaller pay increase than they were seeking in order to help the company avoid raising prices on steel due to inflation and overseas competition. However, after accepting the union's sacrifice, Blough announced a price increase anyway.

Here was an opportunity to study both sides of an issue: I went to the biggest news stand in Kansas City and bought copies of every big city American Sunday paper they had. I flagged each paper's news stories on the Kennedy-Blough argument, and flagged their editorials. On Monday, and for the rest of the week, class time went into preparing summaries of the two sides' arguments. With minor guidance from me, they did it all on their own: they taped stories on walls and windows all over the room, and then we divided into two groups with each assigned to study and organize the arguments from the Kennedy or Blough point of view. There wasn't a winner; there wasn't a loser. The students saw that legitimate arguments could be made to support either side. Because it was a working-class school, their sympathies were mostly with Kennedy and the union, but in the pleasant glow of forty-some year-old memory, they learned by teaching themselves.

In 1962 I'd never heard of Mark Twain's concept of "corn-pone opinions," but I encouraged those journalism students to ask themselves whose interests were being served by the newspaper articles. In retrospect, I realize that, by choosing to cite the facts and arguments that are being presented, I was encouraging them to analyze facts and arguments at least partly by asking, "Whose ox is being gored here?" What are the corn-pone interests the writer is serving by making these arguments?

I am still teaching myself to unlearn my racism. As a pedestrian and a bus and subway rider in New York City, I see a variety of behaviors on every trip I make. I've taught myself to observe the fact that good and bad manners, generosity, selfishness, and sheer common courtesy are in no way tied to ethnicity. I try to apply a humanistic approach to issues like affirmative action in hiring and educational admissions—asking myself what are the corn-pone issues here? Is there justice on both sides? If I settle on a point of view, what is the corn-pone source that has influenced my opinion most?

I sometimes find myself holding opinions that are unpopular with people with whom I'd normally identify. Immigration has been an issue on which I disagree with some of my liberal associates. I believe multi-ethnic immigration is a terrific thing, and I'd like the U.S. to open our doors wider, bringing in many more people from all over the world; but I want to do it systematically and legally. Along with letting many more people enter the country and progress toward citizenship, I want us to fund significant programs of teaching English as a second language in schools and at work places. Maybe it's my German, Pritner grandparents influencing me to try to make things systematic and fair. I want everyone to get in a line and wait their turns. I want to give an equal opportunity to everyone for whom we open our doors. So I struggle every day to come to evaluate social issues while at the same time keeping an eye on the unexpected pockets of racism I still find in my soul.

When I look back over my life, I do see certain patterns that might be applied more broadly to the process of unlearning racism, no matter how unique each person's journey is ultimately. For instance, it was easy for me to remain unconcerned about racial matters as long as my experiences didn't require me to actually get to know any African Americans on a personal basis. I could laugh when a buddy threw an egg at a old black man because I didn't know him, and I didn't know what his life was like. He was a target, not a human being.

It wasn't until I was in the Army that I had the opportunity to listen to an African American describe what his life was really like, and I found my stereotypes being shattered. This first glimmer of understanding was deepened when I was in graduate school living in housing that once again brought me into day-to-day contact, and again I got a glimpse of another's reality.

So it concerns me that American society seems to be becoming more and more segregated again, with gated communities in real estate and schooling, and gated intellectual communities in social media. With the end of the military draft, one common opportunity for people to encounter people unlike themselves disappeared. Without my experiences in the military, I wonder whether I'd have started the unlearning process.

I also find myself wondering to what extent my openness to hearing my fellow soldier's story was affected by the fact that I was also reading Clarence Darrow's autobiography, an autobiography that showed me the heroism of a life committed to standing up for the oppressed. What about the plays, films, and television shows that I saw—how did they affect my views on race? I echo the words of Nigerian novelist Chimimanda Ngozi Adichi, who, in her oft-viewed TED talk, warned of the "danger of a single story." The importance of a multiplicity of voices representing the experiences, thoughts, and feelings of many types of people is so important to the unlearning process.

It is hard to underestimate the effect of enlightened leadership open to challenge and committed to questioning. How might I have been changed if President Braden hadn't come to my office to explain his decision not to name the student center after Malcolm X, but instead he had worked to deny me tenure? If my corn-pone had been taken away at that early stage of my career, would I have been less likely to speak out against racism in the future? I like to think not, but I don't know.

And then there's just sheer luck. What if I had never met and married Evamarii? Our marriage has enabled me to learn more than I could otherwise have learned about black culture and about black Americans' lives in our still-racist society.

I'm well past seventy and, as you can see, still learning how to be the person I want to be, the kind of old man who's learned not to be a racist, who's learned from Mark Twain that I can't get where I want to go "by another man's road."[56] My pride is that I've developed the habit of applying the corn-pone test, especially when I encounter an issue involving race. I've taught myself partly by reading Mark Twain, but I blame nothing on him; I walk alone down my own road, unlearning my racism step by step.

Acknowledgements

A big warm hug of thank you to Scott Walters for his careful editing of Calvin's work. I also thank his wife Laura for her understanding support of the time this project demanded.

My family is my support, and for that I thank my amazing United Nations of a family: Juliet, Freddie, Yvette, and Sayda, Peter, Christian, Jay, and Greg, Christopher, Alysha, Patrick, and Adam, Evelyn, Syrita, Jasmine, Major, and Carlito. I live in your love every day.

And a huge thank you to the universe for giving me the good sense to say "yes" when a lovely man, Calvin Lee Pritner, "came a courtin'."

—Evamarii Johnson

With much appreciation to my friend Evamarii Johnson for sharing Calvin's manuscript with me and cheering me on as we worked on it together.

To my wife, Laura, for her support of 25 years, and her encouragement when I took on this project.

And to Calvin Pritner, without whom I would not have had a career in academia. I spent many a pleasant summer evening on the lawn of the Illinois Shakespeare Festival talking with him about teaching, the "Shakespeare Industry," analyzing and directing plays, baseball, and life in general. I hear his voice on every page of this book.

—*Scott Walters*

NOTES

[1] Letter to Jane Lampton Clemens, 24 August 1853, New York, NY. Reprinted in *Mark Twain's Letters*. Ed. Edgar Marquess, Michael B. Frank, and Kenneth M. Sanderson (Berkeley: University of California Press, 1897), p. 4.

[2] Letters, p. 10

[3] Mark Twain. *Mark Twain's Autobiography*. ed. Albert Bigelow Paine (New York: Harper & Brothers, 1924), I, xi.

[4] Mark Twain, "Corn-Pone Opinions," *Collected Tales, Sketches, Speeches & Essays 1891-1910*. ed. Louis J. Budd (New York: Library of America, 1992), pp. 507-511.

[5] Twain, "Corn-Pone Opinions," p. 510.

[6] Twain, The Private History of a Campaign that Failed," *Collected Tales, Sketches, Speeches & Essays 1852-1890*. ed. Louis J. Budd (New York: Library of America, 1992), pp. 863-882.

[7] Mark Twain in "Mark Twain and the Colored Man" as quoted in http://www.twainquotes.com/18650719t.html

[8] Mark Twain, *The Innocents Abroad, or The New Pilgrims Progress* (New York: New American Library, 1966), p. 40.

[9] Mark Twain, *Roughing It* (New York: New American Library, 1962), p. 118.

¹⁰ Attributed to Mark Twain, Buffalo, NY, *Express*, August 26, 1869. Quoted from: The Buffalonian: http://www.buffalonian.com/hnews/1869onlya nigger.html

¹¹ The octagonal building has been removed to the campus of Elmira College which maintains a center for Mark Twain studies.

¹² Mark Twain letter to William Dean Howells, June 1872, in *Selected Mark Twain – Howells Letters 1872-1910*, ed. Fredrick Anderson, William M. Gibson, and Henry Nash Smith (New York: Atheneum, 1968), p. 9.

¹³ Justin Kaplan, *Mr. Clemens and Mark Twain*, p. 181.

¹⁴ William L. Van Deburg. *Slavery & Race in American Popular Culture* (Madison: University of Wisconsin Press, 1984), pp. 93-94.

¹⁵ Tom Quirk. *Mark Twain: A Study of the Short Fiction* (New York: Twayne Publishers, 1997), p.

¹⁶ Mark Twain. "A True Story, Repeated Word for Word as I Heard It" in *Mark Twain: Collected Tales, Sketches, Speeches, & Essays, 1852-1890*, ed. Louis Budd (New York: The Library of America, 1992), pp. 578-582.

¹⁷ Mark Twain. *Following the Equator: A Journey Around the World.* (New York: Harper & Brothers, 1897), I, 211.

¹⁸ Twain, *Following the Equator,* I, pp. 213-214.

¹⁹ Ibid., p. 162.

²⁰ Twain, *Following the Equator,* II, pp. 28-29.

[21] Mark Twain, in a letter to Twichell, quoted by Powers, p. 593.

[22] Powers, *Mark Twain: A Life* (New York: A Free Press, 2005) pp. 599-600.

[23] Mark Twain, "Mark Twain Home, An Anti-Imperialist," *New York Herald* [New York, October 15, 1900] as quoted by Jim Zwick , ed., ww.boondocksnet.com/ai/twain/mtws_homecoming.html

[24] See also www.boondocksnet.com/ai/twain/index.html for Jim Zwick's editing of Twain's anti-imperialist writings.

[25] Mark Twain in a letter to Dr. Barbour, January 8, 1906, as quoted by Justin Kaplan. *Mr. Clemens and Mark Twain,* (New York: Simon and Schuster, 1966), p. 366.

[26] Mark Twain, "The United States of Lyncherdom," in Kaplan, p. 364. The full text of "The United States of Lyncherdom" is available in *Mark Twain: Collected Tales and Sketches, 1891-1901,* p. 479.

[27] Mark Twain, letter to Frank Bliss in Kaplan, p. 365.

[28] C. Vann Woodward, *The Strange Career of Jim Crow,* 3rd ed. revised (New York: Oxford University Press, 1974), p. 51.

[29] Woodward, p. 56.

[30] Mark Twain as quoted by Bernard DeVoto, *Mark Twain in Eruption: Hitherto Unpublished Pages about Men*

and Events, ed. Bernard DeVoto (New York: Capricorn Books, 1968), p. 380.

31 John S. Tuckey, ed. *Mark Twain's Which Was the Dream and Other Symbolic Writings of the Later Years* (Berkeley: University of California Press, 1968), p. 20.

32 Eisenhower as quoted by Warren in J. Ronald Oakley's *God's Country: America in the Fifties* (New York: Published by Red Dembner Enterprises Corp., Distributed by W. W. Norton & Company, 1990), pp. 194-195.

33 David Caute. The Great Fear: The Anti-Communist Purge Under Truman and Eisenhower (New York: Simon and Schuster, 1978) pp. 416 and 421.

34 Zinn, Howard. *A People's History of the United States: 1492 — Present.* New York: Harper-Collins, 2001. P. 207.

35 Mark Twain, "The Noble Red Man" in *Mark Twain: Collected Tales, Sketches, Speeches, & Essays 1852-1890.* ed. Louis J. Budd (New York: The Library of America), 1992. pp. 442-446.

36 Mark Twain, "Fenimore Cooper's Literary Offences" [sic.] and "Fenimore Cooper's Further Literary Offences" in *Mark Twain: Collected Tales, Sketches, Speeches & Essays 1891-1910.* ed. Louis J. Budd (New York: The Library of America), 1992), pp. 180-200.

37 Mark Twain. Letter to William Dean Howells, cited as "Clemens to Howells [June 1872], in *Selected Mark Twain-Howells Letters,* ed. Frederick Anderson, William M. Gibson, and Henry Nash Smith. New York: Athenaeum, 1968. p. 9.

38 Mark Twain. Letter to Henry Huttleston Rogers, June 18, 1896, as quoted by Robert Cooper. *Around the World with*

with Mark Twain. New York: Arcade Publishing Company, (2000). pp. 298-299

39 Mark Twain. Preface to *Mark Twain's Autobiography,* ed. Albert Bigelow Paine. New York: Harper & Brothers (1924), I, p. xv.

40 Mark Twain. *The Autobiography of Mark Twain.* ed. Charles Neider. New York: Harper & Row (1959), p. 63.

41 S. L. Clemens (Mark Twain), quoted from an unpublished manuscript in the Mark Twain Papers, Berkeley, by Shelley Fishkin in *Lighting Out for the Territory: Reflections on Mark Twain and American Culture.* (New York: Oxford University Press, 1996), p. 101.

42 Fishkin, p. 98.

43 William Dean Howells, *"My Mark Twain,"* (Minneola, NY: Dover Publications, 1997; originally published by Harper & Brothers, 1910), p. 34.

44 Mark Twain quoted by Shelley Fishkin from an unpublished manuscript in the Mark Twain Papers titled, "A Family Sketch," in Fishkin's book, *Was Huck Black? Mark Twain and African American Voices,* (New York: Oxford University Press, 1993), p. 124.

45 Ibid.

46 Ron Powers. *Mark Twain: A Life* (New York: A Free Press, 2005), p. 407.

47 Nat Hentoff, "Introduction" to Mark Twain's *Tom Sawyer Abroad.* The Oxford Mark Twain, ed. Shelley Fisher Fishkin. (New York: Oxford University Press, 1996), p. xxxv.

48 Mark Twain, *The Tragedy of Pudd'nhead Wilson and the Comedy of Those Extraordinary Twins*. The Oxford Mark Twain, ed. Shelley Fisher Fishkin. (New York: Oxford University Press, 1996).

49 "Lynching by Year and Race," November 20, 2005: http://www.law.umkc.edu/faculty/projects/ftrials/shipp/lynchingyear.html. Official numbers of lynchings were not maintained during the late nineteenth and early twentieth centuries.

50 Powers, p. 589

51 Mark Twain. "Stirring Times in Austria," in *The Man Who Corrupted Hadleyburg and Other Stories and Essays,* The Oxford Mark Twain, ed. by Shelley Fisher Fishkin (New York: Oxford University Press, 1996), p. 324.

52 Mark Twain. "Concerning the Jews," in *The Man Who Corrupted Hadleyburg and Other Stories and Essays*. pp. 253-254.

53 Twain, "Concerning the Jews," pp. 268-269.

54 Sadly, Coogan's succumbed to the economic distress brought about by the 2020 coronavirus and has closed.

55 "Song of the South," New Georgia Encyclopedia, http://www.georgiaencyclopedia.org/nge/Article.jsp?id=h-2428

56http://etext.virginia.edu/etcbin/toccernew2?id=TwaSeve.sgm&images=images/modeng&data=/texts/english/modeng/parsed&tag=public&part=all

CPSIA information can be obtained
at www.ICGtesting.com
Printed in the USA
LVHW091732180821
695569LV00010B/473/J